FOLLOW TO
LEAD

Follow Well. Lead Boldly.

TONY RIVERA JR.

Follow To Lead

Paperback ISBN: 979-8-89786-007-4
Hardcover ISBN: 979-8-89786-006-7
eBook ISBN: 979-8-89786-012-8

Unless otherwise indicated, Scripture quotations are taken from the Holy Bible, New International Version®, NIV®.
Copyright © 1973, 1978, 1984, 2011 by Biblica, Inc.™
Used by permission. All rights reserved worldwide.

Cover & Interior design by Pinpoint Publishing

Printed in the United States of America
First Edition: 2025

Pinpoint PUBLISHING
Atlanta, GA
www.Pinpoint.pub

Contents

DEDICATION

The journey of writing Follow to Lead has been one of reflection, gratitude, and deep conviction. This book is not merely a collection of thoughts on leadership and followership; it is the result of a lifetime of experience in ministry, shaped by those who took a chance on me, invested in me, and modeled the principles of servant leadership that I now seek to pass on to others.

First and foremost, I am profoundly grateful to my spiritual parents, the late Bishop Tony Miller and Pastor Kathy Miller. Their unwavering faith in me, their wisdom, and their example of servant-hearted leadership changed the course of my life. They saw in me a heart willing to serve, and in doing so, they positioned me to grow into the leader God was shaping me to be. Their legacy continues to inspire me every day.

To my parents, Tony ("Papi") and Rosa ("Mami") Rivera, I owe an immeasurable debt of gratitude. They lived what they taught, leading by example in both faith and service. Through their lives, I witnessed the beauty and power of servant leadership long before I ever had words to articulate it. Their love, sacrifice, and faithfulness laid the foundation upon which I stand today.

To my community of faith, Citi Church Miami, thank you for your willingness to follow the vision of disciples making disciples. Your faithfulness and dedication to the call of Christ are a testament to what happens when leaders and followers work together in unity. You have shown me time and time again that the Church is at its best when leadership is not about position or power but about serving and elevating others.

To my family—my greatest source of strength and encouragement. To my wife, Dianna, my partner of 32 years, your love,
wisdom, and steadfast support have been my anchor in every
season. Your faith and perseverance inspire me daily. To my
daughter, Makenzie, thank you for embracing this journey, for
living out the calling, and for reminding me that true leadership
begins at home.

Above all, I dedicate this work to my Lord and Savior, Jesus
Christ—the greatest leader, the greatest servant, and the
greatest example of followership. His life, His teachings, and
His sacrifice are the foundation of everything I have learned
about leadership. It is my prayer that this book will not only
challenge you but also inspire you to walk the path of true
discipleship—the kind of followership that leads to transformation, multiplication, and a life fully surrendered to God's purpose.

May this book encourage you to follow well so that you may
lead well, and in doing so, advance His Kingdom on earth.

With gratitude and expectation,

Tony Rivera Jr.

INTRODUCTION:

The Death of Leadership and the Rise of Followership

The Concept of Leadership: A Modern Enterprise

The concept of leadership as we understand it today is a relatively modern construct. Historically, leadership was often seen as a divine right or a role assigned by birth, particularly in the context of monarchies and religious institutions. Ancient societies typically viewed leadership as something ordained by God or as an inherent aspect of royalty. For example, the concept of the "divine right of kings" was prevalent in medieval Europe, where kings ruled with the belief that their authority was granted directly by God.[1]

During the Enlightenment, this understanding began to shift as ideas of democracy and individual rights emerged. Philosophers like John Locke and Jean-Jacques Rousseau challenged the notion of divinely ordained leadership, arguing instead that legitimate political authority arose from the consent of the governed.[2] This shift laid the groundwork for modern democratic systems, where leadership is seen as a role conferred by the people rather than by divine mandate.

In the 20th century, leadership became increasingly professionalized, particularly in the corporate world. The rise of management sciences and leadership theories in the mid-20th century brought new focus to the skills, behaviors, and strategies that define effective leadership. Scholars like Peter Drucker and Warren Bennis played pivotal roles in shaping modern leadership theory, emphasizing the importance of vision, communication, and organizational culture in effective leadership.[3]

Today, the leadership enterprise is often characterized by an emphasis on personal branding, charisma, and influence. This focus on the individual leader can sometimes overshadow the collective aspects of leadership, such as the role of followers in the success of a leader or the ethical responsibilities of leadership.[4] This modern perspective raises important questions about the sustainability and morality of leadership models that prioritize individual success over communal well-being.

From Divine Mandate to Democratic Leadership

The evolution of leadership from a divine mandate to a role within democratic societies reflects broader shifts in human thought and governance. In ancient times, leaders were often chosen by what was perceived as divine will. This is evident in biblical accounts of kings like Saul, David, and Solomon, whose leadership was established through divine selection as described in the Old Testament.[5]

With the rise of nation-states and the influence of Enlightenment thinking, the divine right of kings gradually gave way to the concept of sovereignty residing with the people. The American and French revolutions were pivotal in this transition, as they established new forms of government based on democratic principles. These revolutions were heavily influenced by Enlightenment thinkers who advocated for the rights of individuals and the accountability of leaders to the people.[6]

In this new paradigm, leadership became less about divine favor and more about the consent of the governed. Leaders were now expected to serve the will of the people, embodying the ideals of democracy, such as equality, justice, and representation. This shift fundamentally changed the nature of leadership, making it more accessible yet also more complex, as leaders were now accountable not only to a higher power but also to their constituents.[7]

The Rise of Followership: A Necessary Evolution

As leadership has evolved, so too has the concept of followership. Historically, followers were often seen as passive recipients of a leader's decisions. However, contemporary scholarship increasingly recognizes that followership is an active, dynamic role that is crucial to the success of any leadership endeavor. Scholars like Robert Kelley and Barbara Kellerman have been instrumental in bringing attention to the importance of followership, arguing that followers are not merely subordinates but key players in the leadership process.[8]

Kelley, in particular, introduced the idea of "exemplary followership," where followers are independent, critical thinkers who actively engage with and support their leaders in achieving common goals.[9] This concept challenges traditional hierarchies and emphasizes the collaborative nature of leadership and followership. Kellerman further expands on this by highlighting the power and influence that followers can wield, particularly in the digital age where social media platforms have given rise to movements led by grassroots followership rather than traditional leadership structures.[10]

This shift in perspective is increasingly relevant in today's world, where the lines between leaders and followers are often blurred. In many organizations, followers play a significant role in shaping strategies, driving innovation, and holding leaders accountable. As a result, the success of leadership is increasingly seen as dependent not just on the leader's abilities but also on the engagement and effectiveness of their followers.[11]

Jesus's Model of Servant Leadership and Followership

Amid these evolving ideas of leadership and followership, the model presented by Jesus Christ stands out as both timeless and transformative. Jesus's approach to leadership was radically different from the prevailing models of His time. Rather than seeking power or authority, Jesus emphasized servanthood, humility, and self-sacrifice. His leadership was characterized by a deep commitment to serving others, as exemplified in His washing of the disciples' feet (John 13:1-17) and His teaching that "the Son of Man did not come to be served, but to serve, and to give his life as a ransom for many" (Mark 10:45).[12]

Jesus also modeled followership in His relationship with the Father, demonstrating obedience and submission to God's will. His life and ministry exemplified the principle that true leadership is rooted in followership—following God's direction and serving others. This model has profound implications for both leaders and followers in the Church today, as it challenges the conventional notions of power and authority, calling instead for a leadership and followership grounded in love, humility, and service.[13]

As we explore the themes of leadership and followership in this book, Jesus's example will serve as a guiding principle, offering insights into how we can develop more ethical, effective, and spiritually grounded approaches to leadership in the modern world.

CHAPTER ONE:

The Evolution of Leadership – From Divine Mandate to Democratic Ideals

Introduction

Leadership, as we understand it today, is the result of a long and complex evolution. Historically, leadership was often seen as a role ordained by divine mandate, especially in monarchies and religious institutions. Over time, this understanding shifted, particularly during the Enlightenment, when the ideas of democracy and individual rights began to take hold. This chapter explores the evolution of leadership from ancient times to the modern era, tracing the transition from divine authority to democratic ideals and examining how these changes have shaped contemporary leadership models.

Leadership in Ancient Times – Divine Right and Sovereignty

In ancient civilizations, leadership was frequently viewed as a divine right. Kings and rulers were often considered to be chosen by the gods, and their authority was seen as unquestionable. This concept of the divine right of kings is perhaps most famously associated with European monarchies during the medieval and early modern periods, but it has roots that extend back to ancient Mesopotamia, Egypt, and China.[1]

For instance, the Pharaohs of ancient Egypt were considered to be gods in human form, ruling with absolute power as intermediaries between the gods and the people.[2] Similarly, in Mesopotamian culture, kings like Hammurabi were seen as divinely appointed, with their laws and decrees carrying the weight of divine sanction.[3] This belief in the divine right of rulers was also prevalent in ancient Israel, where kings such as Saul, David, and Solomon were anointed by prophets as chosen by God.[4]

The Transition to Sovereignty – The Rise of Monarchies

As societies became more complex, the roles of kings and leaders expanded beyond religious functions to include governance, lawmaking, and military command. The concept of sovereignty—where the ruler holds supreme power within a territory—became more formalized. This was evident in the legal codes established by rulers such as Hammurabi, whose famous code was one of the earliest examples of a ruler codifying laws based on divine authority.[5]

In Europe, the divine right of kings became a central doctrine in the governance of medieval and early modern states. Monarchs like Louis XIV of France epitomized this belief, famously declaring, "L'état, c'est moi" (I am the state), which reflected the idea that the king's authority was absolute and divinely ordained.[6] This belief was used to justify the centralization of power and the suppression of dissent, as questioning the king's authority was equated with questioning God.

The Enlightenment – The Shift to Democratic Leadership

The Enlightenment brought about a significant shift in the understanding of leadership and authority. Enlightenment thinkers such as John Locke, Jean-Jacques Rousseau, and Montesquieu challenged the idea of the divine right of kings and argued for the sovereignty of the people.[7] Locke's theory of the social contract proposed that legitimate political authority arises from the consent of the governed, not from divine mandate. This idea laid the groundwork for modern democratic thought and the eventual decline of monarchies in favor of republics and constitutional governments.[8]

Rousseau's concept of the "general will" further developed the idea that political authority should reflect the collective will of the people rather than the desires of a single ruler.[9] Montesquieu's advocacy for the separation of powers became a foundational principle for many modern democracies, ensuring that no single branch of government could dominate the others.[10] These Enlightenment ideals were instrumental in shaping the political revolutions of the 18th century, particularly in America and France, where the overthrow of monarchies and the establishment of republics were seen as the realization of these new principles of leadership.[11]

The Modern Leadership Paradigm – Professionalization and Individualism

In the 20th century, leadership became increasingly professionalized, particularly in the corporate and political spheres. The rise of management sciences and leadership theories brought new focus to the skills, behaviors, and strategies that define effective leadership. Scholars like Peter Drucker emphasized the importance of management as a distinct function that requires specialized knowledge and skills.[12] Drucker's work, particularly in *The Practice of Management*, helped to establish leadership as a discipline in its own right, distinct from but closely related to management.[13]

Warren Bennis, another influential leadership scholar, highlighted the difference between leadership and management, famously stating, "Managers do things right; leaders do the right thing."[14] Bennis's work emphasized the importance of vision, communication, and the ability to inspire others, qualities that are often associated with transformational leadership. This period also saw the rise of charismatic leadership, where a leader's personal appeal and ability to inspire loyalty became central to their effectiveness.[15]

Today, leadership is often viewed through the lens of individualism, where personal branding, charisma, and influence are seen as key attributes. This focus on the individual leader can sometimes overshadow the collective aspects of leadership, such as the role of followers and the ethical responsibilities of leadership.[16] As a result, modern leadership models often emphasize the importance of adaptability, emotional intelligence, and the ability to navigate complex social dynamics.[17]

Conclusion: The Evolving Nature of Leadership

The evolution of leadership from divine mandate to democratic ideals reflects broader shifts in human thought and society. As we continue to grapple with the complexities of leadership in the modern world, it is important to remember that leadership is not just about the individual at the top. It is a dynamic process that involves both leaders and followers working together toward a common goal.

As we explore the themes of leadership and followership in this book, we will consider how these historical developments have shaped our current understanding of leadership and how we can apply these lessons to create more ethical, effective, and sustainable leadership models in our communities and organizations.

Discussion Questions

1.   How did the concept of the divine right of kings shape leadership and governance in ancient and medieval societies? How does this compare to modern democratic ideals?

2.   Reflect on the transition from leadership as a divine mandate to leadership based on the consent of the governed. How has this shift impacted the way we view authority and leadership today?

3.   What were the key contributions of Enlightenment thinkers like John Locke and Jean-Jacques Rousseau to the evolution of leadership? How do their ideas continue to influence leadership in modern democratic societies?

4.   Consider the role of the social contract and the separation of powers in shaping modern leadership. How do these concepts ensure accountability and ethical governance?

5.   In what ways has the professionalization of leadership in the 20th century changed our expectations of leaders? What are the potential benefits and drawbacks of viewing leadership through the lens of management science?

6.   Discuss the impact of scholars like Peter Drucker and Warren Bennis on our understanding of leadership. How do their theories align with or challenge traditional views of leadership?

7.   How does the modern focus on individualism and personal branding in leadership differ from earlier models of lead-

ership? What are the implications of this shift for both leaders and followers?

8.   Analyze the rise of charismatic leadership and personal branding in contemporary society. How does this focus on the individual leader affect the collective aspects of leadership?

9.   Considering the historical evolution of leadership, what lessons can we apply to developing more ethical and sustainable leadership models today?

10.   Reflect on how understanding the history of leadership can inform our approach to leadership in the present. What principles from the past should be preserved, and what should be re-evaluated?

11.   How does the relationship between leaders and followers influence the effectiveness of leadership? What role should followers play in ensuring ethical and accountable leadership?

12.   Explore the dynamic between leaders and followers, considering the importance of mutual responsibility. How can followers contribute to ethical leadership in their communities and organizations?

CHAPTER TWO:

The Sovereignty of Kings – Leadership by Birthright and Conquest

Introduction

Leadership by birthright and conquest has been a fundamental aspect of governance throughout much of human history. Kingship, often rooted in the divine right or established through military conquest, has shaped the structure of societies and the nature of authority for centuries. This chapter delves into how these forms of leadership developed, their implications on governance and society, and how these ancient concepts continue to influence modern ideas about leadership and power.

Leadership by Birthright – The Divine Right of Kings

The concept of the divine right of kings was a powerful doctrine in many ancient and medieval societies. It asserted that monarchs were chosen by God and ruled with divine sanction. This belief gave kings both political and religious authority, making their leadership not only a matter of governance but of spiritual significance as well. In medieval Europe, this idea was formalized through elaborate coronation rituals where kings were anointed with holy oil, symbolizing their sacred role.[1]

For instance, the French kings were known as the "Most Christian King" (Rex Christianissimus), a title that reflected their perceived divine favor and special relationship with the Church.[2] The stability of these monarchies depended heavily on the belief that the royal bloodline was sanctified by God, making any challenge to the king's authority not just a political rebellion but a blasphemous act against divine order.[3]

This concept was not confined to Europe. In ancient Egypt, the Pharaohs were believed to be gods incarnate—specifically, the living Horus, the god of the sky and the son of Osiris and Isis. The Pharaoh was both a political leader and a divine figure who maintained Ma'at—the order and balance of the universe—through his rule.[4] Similarly, in China, the Mandate of Heaven was a principle that granted emperors the right to rule based on their ability to govern well and fairly. Unlike the divine right in Europe, the Mandate of Heaven could be revoked by heaven if a ruler became despotic or failed to fulfill his duties, leading to his overthrow and the rise of a new dynasty.[5]

Leadership by Conquest – The Power of the Sword

While birthright provided a basis for leadership in many cultures, conquest was another primary means through which power was attained and legitimized. Leadership by conquest was characterized by the use of military force to establish dominance, often leading to the creation of empires and new dynasties. Conquerors not only seized power but often sought to legitimize their rule through various means, including religion, law, and culture.

One of the most iconic examples of leadership by conquest is Alexander the Great, who, by the age of 30, had created one of the largest empires in history, stretching from Greece to Egypt and as far east as India.[6] Alexander's conquests were not just about territorial expansion; they were also about spreading Hellenistic culture, which blended Greek, Persian, Egyptian, and Indian elements. This cultural integration helped solidify his empire and maintain control over diverse populations.

Similarly, the Mongol Empire, under the leadership of Genghis Khan, expanded across Asia and into Europe through a series of brutal and highly strategic military campaigns. Genghis Khan's leadership was marked by his ability to unite the Mongol tribes and create a code of law, known as Yassa, which helped maintain order within his vast empire.[z] His conquests not only reshaped the political landscape of Asia but also facilitated trade and cultural exchange along the Silk Road.

In the biblical context, the concept of leadership by conquest is illustrated in the story of King David, who, after uniting the tribes of Israel, expanded his kingdom through military victories over neighboring nations. David's leadership, however, was not solely based on his military prowess; it was also seen as divinely ordained, as evidenced by his anointing by the prophet Samuel and the covenant established with God that promised the continuation of his dynasty.[8]

The Impact of Birthright and Conquest on Society

Leadership by birthright and conquest had profound implications for the societies governed by such rulers. These forms of leadership often led to the establishment of rigid class structures, where power and privilege were concentrated in the hands of a few. In many cases, this created a significant divide between the ruling elite and the general populace, with social mobility being severely restricted.

In medieval Europe, for example, the feudal system entrenched the power of the nobility, who were often related to or directly descended from the ruling monarch. This system created a hierarchy where loyalty and service to the king were rewarded with land and titles, further reinforcing the notion that leadership and privilege were tied to birthright.[9]

Conquest, on the other hand, often led to the subjugation of conquered peoples and the imposition of new cultural and legal systems. This could result in significant social and cultural changes, as seen in the Roman Empire, where conquered territories were integrated into the Roman state and subjected to Roman law and customs. While this often brought about greater administrative efficiency and economic development, it also led to the erosion of local traditions and identities.[10]

However, both birthright and conquest also provided a sense of stability and continuity, especially in times of uncertainty. The idea that a ruler was chosen by the gods or had proven themselves through conquest could legitimize their authority and provide a unifying figure for a diverse population. This was particularly important in empires like that of the Persians under Cyrus the Great, who used both his royal lineage and his reputation as a just conqueror to establish a stable and prosperous empire.[11]

The Legacy of Birthright and Conquest in Modern Leadership

While the explicit rule by birthright and conquest has largely faded in most parts of the world, the legacies of these concepts remain evident in contemporary leadership structures. Modern monarchies, though mostly ceremonial, still evoke the idea of leadership by birthright, with royal families often serving as symbols of national unity and continuity. Similarly, the concept of conquest has evolved into more subtle forms, such as economic and cultural domination, where powerful nations or corporations exert influence over others through non-military means.

Moreover, the historical examples of leadership by birthright and conquest continue to shape how we perceive authority and power. Leaders who rise to prominence through their achievements, whether in business, politics, or other fields, often draw parallels to the conquerors of old, with their success being seen as a justification for their authority. The notion of "earning" leadership through conquest—be it literal or metaphorical—remains a powerful narrative in the modern world.

Conclusion

The sovereignty of kings, whether established by birthright or conquest, played a crucial role in shaping the history and governance of many societies. These forms of leadership provided both stability and continuity, but also reinforced social hierarchies and, at times, led to significant social and cultural upheaval. Understanding the historical context of these leadership models helps us to better appreciate the complexities of power and authority, both in the past and in the present.

As we continue to explore the evolution of leadership in this book, it is essential to recognize the enduring influence of these ancient concepts. Whether through the symbolic power of modern monarchies or the competitive spirit of contemporary leaders, the legacies of birthright and conquest continue to shape our understanding of leadership and its role in society.

Discussion Questions

1.   How did the concept of the divine right of kings influence the governance and social structure of medieval Europe? What parallels can you draw between this historical concept and modern leadership models?

2.   Reflect on how the belief in divinely ordained leadership affected both the authority of rulers and the social hierarchy. Consider how these ideas might still be reflected in contemporary leadership, particularly in political or religious contexts.

3.   In what ways did leaders like Alexander the Great and Genghis Khan use conquest to legitimize their rule? How did their conquests shape the societies they governed?

4.   Discuss the methods these leaders used to consolidate power and the long-term effects of their conquests on the cultures and economies of their empires. How does the idea of "conquest" manifest in modern leadership?

5.   The Mandate of Heaven in China allowed for the overthrow of rulers who failed in their duties. How does this concept compare to modern ideas of leadership accountability?

6.   Explore the similarities between the Mandate of Heaven and contemporary mechanisms for holding leaders accountable, such as democratic elections or impeachment processes. What can we learn from this ancient concept about maintaining ethical leadership today?

7.   What are the lasting legacies of leadership by birthright and conquest in today's world? How do these ancient concepts continue to influence modern ideas about authority and power?

8.   Consider how the notions of inherited power and "earned" leadership through achievement still play a role in modern society, particularly in the realms of politics, business,

and royalty. How do these legacies affect our expectations of leaders?

9.   How did the concept of birthright leadership create social stability, and in what ways did it reinforce social in-equalities? What lessons can we draw from this for addressing inequality in modern leadership structures?

10.   Discuss the dual role of birthright in providing continu-ity while also perpetuating social divisions. How can we apply these lessons to create more inclusive and equitable leader-ship today?

11.   Reflect on the biblical examples of leadership by birth-right and conquest, such as the stories of King David and Solo-mon. How do these stories inform our understanding of divine authority and leadership?

12.   Analyze the role of divine selection and military con-quest in the establishment of Israel's monarchy. How do these narratives shape our theological understanding of leadership and its responsibilities?

CHAPTER THREE:

The Enlightenment and the Democratization of Leadership

Introduction

The Enlightenment was a period of profound intellectual and philosophical development in the 17th and 18th centuries, which fundamentally changed the way people thought about leadership, governance, and authority. It marked the transition from leadership based on divine right and hereditary succession to leadership grounded in democratic principles and the consent of the governed. This chapter examines the key ideas and figures of the Enlightenment that contributed to this transformation and explores how these ideas influenced modern concepts of leadership and followership.

The Enlightenment and the Birth of Modern Political Thought

The Enlightenment, often referred to as the "Age of Reason," was characterized by an emphasis on reason, individualism, and skepticism toward traditional authority. Thinkers of this period questioned the legitimacy of monarchs who claimed divine right to rule and instead promoted the idea that all people had inherent rights and that legitimate leadership must be based on the consent of the governed.

John Locke and the Social Contract

One of the most influential Enlightenment thinkers was John Locke, whose ideas about government and leadership were revolutionary. Locke argued that all individuals possess natural rights to life, liberty, and property, and that the primary purpose of government is to protect these rights. He introduced the concept of the social contract, where individuals consent to be governed in exchange for the protection of their rights.[1]

Locke's ideas directly challenged the notion of the divine right of kings, proposing instead that political authority arises from the people. This shift laid the groundwork for the development of modern democracies, where leadership is seen as a role conferred by the people rather than by God or birthright.[2]

Montesquieu and the Separation of Powers

Another key figure of the Enlightenment was Montesquieu, whose work *The Spirit of the Laws* argued for the separation of powers within government. Montesquieu believed that dividing government authority among different branches—legislative, executive, and judicial—was essential to preventing tyranny and ensuring freedom.[3]

Montesquieu's ideas were foundational in the development of constitutional governments, particularly in the United States, where the Constitution established a system of checks and balances that reflected his principles. This separation of powers not only democratized leadership by limiting the power of any one leader or branch of government but also underscored the importance of accountability in leadership.[4]

Rousseau and the General Will

Jean-Jacques Rousseau, another prominent Enlightenment thinker, introduced the concept of the "general will," which he described in his work *The Social Contract*. Rousseau argued that true sovereignty belongs to the people, who collectively express their will through laws and government actions that reflect the common good.[5]

Rousseau's ideas further democratized the concept of leadership by emphasizing that legitimate leaders must act in accordance with the general will of the people, rather than their own interests. This notion of the general will became a guiding principle for many democratic revolutions, including the French Revolution, and continues to influence modern democratic theory.[6]

The Impact of Enlightenment Ideas on Leadership

The Enlightenment's emphasis on reason, individual rights, and the social contract profoundly changed how leadership was understood and practiced. These ideas contributed to the decline of absolute monarchies and the rise of republics and constitutional monarchies, where leaders were accountable to the people.

The American Revolution

The American Revolution was one of the first major political movements to be directly influenced by Enlightenment ideas. The Founding Fathers, including Thomas Jefferson and James Madison, were deeply influenced by the writings of Locke, Montesquieu, and Rousseau.[7] The Declaration of Independence, which articulated the colonies' reasons for seeking independence from Britain, drew heavily on Locke's ideas about natural rights and the social contract.[8]

The Constitution that followed established a government based on the principles of democracy, separation of powers, and the rule of law. This new form of leadership, grounded in Enlightenment principles, was a radical departure from the hereditary monarchy that had previously governed the colonies.

The French Revolution

The French Revolution was another significant event that was deeply influenced by Enlightenment thought. The revolutionaries sought to overthrow the absolute monarchy of Louis XVI and establish a government based on the principles of liberty, equality, and fraternity.[9]

Rousseau's concept of the general will was particularly influential during the Revolution, as the new leaders sought to create a society where the government acted in the interests of the people. However, the Revolution also illustrated the challenges of implementing Enlightenment ideals in practice, as the pursuit of the general will sometimes led to extreme measures and the erosion of individual rights during the Reign of Terror.[10]

The Legacy of the Enlightenment in Modern Leadership

The ideas of the Enlightenment continue to influence modern concepts of leadership and governance. The emphasis on reason, individual rights, and the rule of law remains central to democratic societies today. Leaders are expected to be accountable to the people, to govern in accordance with the law, and to respect the rights of individuals.

In addition, the Enlightenment's focus on the importance of education and informed citizenry has shaped modern views on the role of followers in leadership. In a democratic society, followers are not passive subjects but active participants in the political process, capable of holding leaders accountable and contributing to the direction of government.[11]

Conclusion

The Enlightenment marked a pivotal shift in the way leadership was conceived and practiced. By challenging the traditional notions of divine right and hereditary rule, Enlightenment thinkers laid the groundwork for modern democratic leadership. Their ideas continue to resonate today, influencing how we understand the relationship between leaders and followers and the principles that should guide those in positions of power.

As we continue to explore the evolution of leadership in this book, it is essential to consider how these Enlightenment ideas can inform our current practices and help us create more just and effective leadership models in our communities and organizations.

Discussion Questions

1.   How did John Locke's concept of the social contract challenge the traditional notion of the divine right of kings? How is this concept reflected in modern democratic societies?

2.   Reflect on how Locke's ideas shifted the basis of political authority from divine right to the consent of the governed. Consider how this shift influences contemporary views on leadership and governance.

3.   Montesquieu's advocacy for the separation of powers has been influential in the design of many modern governments. How does this principle help prevent the concentration of power, and why is it important for maintaining democratic leadership?

4.   Discuss the importance of checks and balances in government. How does separating powers between branches of government contribute to effective and ethical leadership?

5.   Rousseau's idea of the general will emphasized that leaders must govern in the interest of the people. How can modern leaders ensure that they are acting in accordance with the general will, and what challenges might they face in doing so?

6.   Explore the concept of the general will and its application in modern leadership. What are the potential conflicts between individual rights and the collective good?

7.   The Enlightenment had a significant impact on both the American and French revolutions. How did Enlightenment ideas shape the leadership structures that emerged from these revolutions?

8.   Compare the outcomes of the American and French revolutions in terms of leadership and governance. How did

The Enlightenment and the Democratization of Leadership

Enlightenment thought guide the creation of new political systems?

9. In what ways do the ideas of the Enlightenment continue to influence leadership and governance today? How can these ideas be applied to address contemporary challenges in leadership?

10. Consider the relevance of Enlightenment principles in modern leadership. How can concepts like the social contract, separation of powers, and the general will inform current leadership practices?

11. The Enlightenment emphasized the role of reason and education in leadership and followership. How can leaders today foster an informed and engaged citizenry or team?

12. Discuss the importance of education and critical thinking in leadership. How can leaders encourage active participation and accountability among their followers?

CHAPTER FOUR:

From Kings to Citizens – The Rise of Democratic Leadership

Introduction

The transition from monarchies to democratic leadership represents one of the most significant shifts in the history of governance. As the Enlightenment ideas of equality, representation, and the rule of law gained traction, the authority of kings began to wane, giving rise to new forms of leadership rooted in the will of the people. This chapter explores the emergence of democratic leadership, examining key historical developments, the philosophical underpinnings of democracy, and how these ideas continue to influence modern leadership structures.

The Decline of Monarchy and the Emergence of Democratic Ideals

The decline of monarchy in Europe and the rise of democratic ideals were driven by a combination of intellectual, social, and political changes. The Enlightenment had already laid the groundwork by challenging the divine right of kings and advocating for the rights of individuals. However, it was the political upheavals of the late 18th and early 19th centuries that accelerated the transition from kings to citizens as the primary source of political authority.

The American Revolution and the Birth of a Republic

The American Revolution (1775–1783) was a pivotal moment in the transition from monarchic to democratic governance. The colonies' rebellion against British rule was motivated by a desire for self-governance and the protection of natural rights, as articulated by Enlightenment thinkers like John Locke.[1] The Declaration of Independence, drafted in 1776, famously asserted that "all men are created equal" and that governments derive "their just powers from the consent of the governed."[2]

The successful establishment of the United States as a republic marked the first major break from traditional monarchical rule in the Western world. The U.S. Constitution, ratified in 1787, created a system of government based on the principles of federalism, separation of powers, and checks and balances. This new form of leadership was revolutionary, not just in its rejection of monarchy, but in its embrace of the idea that leaders should be elected by and accountable to the people.[3]

The French Revolution and the Rise of Popular Sovereignty

The French Revolution (1789–1799) further demonstrated the decline of monarchic power and the rise of democratic ideals. Inspired by both the American Revolution and Enlightenment thought, the French Revolution sought to overthrow the absolute monarchy of Louis XVI and establish a government based on the principles of liberty, equality, and fraternity.[4] The revolutionaries' Declaration of the Rights of Man and of the Citizen, adopted in 1789, enshrined the concept of popular sovereignty and declared that "the source of all sovereignty resides essentially in the nation."[5]

The revolution led to the abolition of the monarchy and the establishment of the First French Republic. However, the revolution also highlighted the challenges of implementing democratic ideals, as the initial push for liberty and equality gave way to the Reign of Terror, during which thousands were executed in the name of preserving the revolution.[6] Despite these challenges, the French Revolution profoundly influenced the spread of democratic ideas across Europe and beyond.

The Industrial Revolution and the Expansion of Democratic Participation

The Industrial Revolution, which began in the late 18th century, brought about significant social and economic changes that further expanded democratic participation. As industrialization led to the growth of cities and the rise of a new middle class, demands for political representation and workers' rights increased. The push for broader suffrage and labor reforms became central issues in many countries, leading to gradual expansions of the electorate and the development of new political movements.

In Britain, for example, the Reform Acts of the 19th century gradually extended the right to vote to a larger portion of the population, moving the country closer to a true representative democracy.[7] Similarly, in the United States, the expansion of suffrage, particularly through the 15th and 19th Amendments, extended voting rights to African Americans and women, respectively, reflecting the growing belief that leadership should be representative of all citizens, not just a privileged few.[8]

The Philosophical Foundations of Democratic Leadership

The transition from kings to citizens was not just a political development but also a philosophical shift in the understanding of leadership and authority. Democratic leadership is rooted in several key principles that continue to guide modern governance.

Equality and Representation

At the heart of democratic leadership is the principle of equality. Unlike monarchies, where power is concentrated in the
hands of a single ruler or a small elite, democracies are based
on the idea that all citizens have an equal say in how they are
governed. This principle is reflected in the concept of representation, where leaders are elected to serve as representatives of the people and are accountable to them.

The idea of representation was heavily influenced by the writings of political theorists like Jean-Jacques Rousseau and Montesquieu. Rousseau's concept of the general will emphasized
that leaders must govern in accordance with the collective will
of the people.[2] Montesquieu's advocacy for the separation of
powers and a system of checks and balances helped ensure
that no single leader or group could dominate the government,
thereby protecting the rights of individuals.[10]

The Rule of Law

Another fundamental principle of democratic leadership is the
rule of law, which asserts that all individuals and institutions,
including leaders, are subject to the law. This principle ensures
that leadership is not arbitrary, but is exercised within a framework of established rules and procedures. The rule of law is
essential for maintaining order and protecting the rights of citizens, as it provides a mechanism for holding leaders accountable and preventing abuses of power.

The importance of the rule of law in democratic leadership
is evident in the U.S. Constitution, which establishes a legal
framework for governance and includes provisions for the
impeachment of leaders who violate their duties.[11] The rule of
law also underpins the concept of constitutionalism, where the
powers of government are limited by a written or unwritten
constitution that guarantees fundamental rights and freedoms.

The Impact of Democratic Leadership on Modern Society

The rise of democratic leadership has had a profound impact on modern society. Democracies have generally been more successful than monarchies in providing for the well-being of their citizens, as they are more responsive to the needs and demands of the people. Democratic leadership has also fostered greater political stability, as leaders who fail to meet the expectations of their constituents can be peacefully removed through elections.

Moreover, democratic leadership has encouraged greater civic participation, as citizens in democracies have the opportunity to engage in the political process through voting, activism, and public discourse. This participation helps to ensure that leaders remain accountable and that government policies reflect the will of the people.

However, democratic leadership is not without its challenges. The increasing polarization of political discourse, the influence of money in politics, and the erosion of public trust in institutions are significant issues facing modern democracies. These challenges underscore the need for ongoing vigilance in protecting democratic principles and ensuring that leadership remains truly representative and accountable.

Conclusion

The transition from kings to citizens marked a fundamental shift in the understanding and practice of leadership. The rise of democratic ideals, rooted in the principles of equality, representation, and the rule of law, has reshaped governance and empowered individuals to take an active role in determining their leaders. As we continue to explore the evolution of leadership in this book, it is essential to recognize the importance of these democratic principles in shaping modern leadership and to consider how they can be upheld and strengthened in the face of contemporary challenges.

Discussion Questions

1.   How did the American and French revolutions contribute to the decline of monarchy and the rise of democratic
leadership? What key principles emerged from these revolutions that continue to influence modern democracies?

2.   Reflect on how the ideas of equality, representation,
and popular sovereignty were embodied in these revolutions
and how they shaped the development of democratic leadership.

3.   In what ways did the Industrial Revolution contribute to
the expansion of democratic participation? How did the social
and economic changes of this period influence the demands
for broader representation and suffrage?

4.   Discuss the connection between industrialization and
the rise of political movements advocating for expanded rights
and representation. How did these movements contribute to
the evolution of democratic leadership?

5.   What are the key philosophical principles underlying
democratic leadership, and how do they differ from the principles of monarchic leadership? How do these principles ensure
accountability and protect individual rights?

6.   Explore the principles of equality, representation, and
the rule of law in democratic leadership. How do these principles help prevent abuses of power and ensure that leadership
remains responsive to the people?

7.   The rule of law is a fundamental principle of democratic
leadership. How does this principle help maintain order and
protect the rights of citizens? What challenges does it face in
contemporary democracies?

8.   Analyze the importance of the rule of law in democratic
societies. What are the potential threats to this principle, and

how can they be addressed to ensure effective and just leadership?

9.   How does the idea of representation shape the relationship between leaders and citizens in a democracy? What are the responsibilities of both leaders and followers in maintaining a healthy democratic system?

10.   Consider the role of elected representatives in a democracy. How should leaders balance the will of the people with the need to make informed decisions? What role do citizens play in holding their leaders accountable?

11.   What challenges do modern democracies face in upholding the principles of democratic leadership? How can these challenges be addressed to ensure that leadership remains representative and accountable?

12.   Discuss contemporary issues such as political polarization, the influence of money in politics, and declining public trust. How can democratic societies work to overcome these challenges and strengthen their leadership structures?

CHAPTER FIVE:

Leadership in the Age of Revolutions – The Transformation of Authority

Introduction

The late 18th and early 19th centuries were marked by a wave of political revolutions that fundamentally transformed leadership and authority. The American, French, and Latin American revolutions, among others, challenged the traditional structures of power and paved the way for modern democratic states. These revolutions redefined what it meant to be a leader, shifting the focus from divine right and hereditary rule to the consent of the governed, individual rights, and the rule of law. This chapter examines how these revolutions contributed to the transformation of leadership and explores the enduring impact of these changes on contemporary governance.

The American Revolution – A New Model of Leadership

The American Revolution (1775–1783) was one of the earliest and most influential events in the Age of Revolutions. The colonists' struggle for independence from British rule was rooted in Enlightenment ideals, particularly the belief in natural rights and the social contract, as articulated by thinkers like John Locke.[1] The revolutionaries sought to create a government that derived its authority from the consent of the governed rather than from monarchic or aristocratic privilege.

George Washington – The Citizen Leader

One of the most significant figures to emerge from the American Revolution was George Washington, who became the embodiment of the new model of leadership. Washington's decision to relinquish power after leading the Continental Army to victory and serving two terms as the first President of the United States set a precedent for peaceful transitions of power and the principle that leadership should be temporary and accountable to the people.[2] Washington's leadership style, characterized by humility, restraint, and a deep commitment to republican ideals, helped shape the identity of the fledgling nation and set a standard for future leaders.

The U.S. Constitution – Institutionalizing Democratic Leadership

The drafting and ratification of the U.S. Constitution in 1787 institutionalized the principles of democratic leadership that had emerged during the revolution. The Constitution established a system of checks and balances, the separation of powers, and federalism, all designed to prevent the concentration of power in any single leader or branch of government.[3] This framework not only provided a blueprint for governance in the United States but also influenced the development of democratic institutions around the world.

The French Revolution – Radical Change and the Reimagining of Leadership

The French Revolution (1789–1799) was even more radical in its challenge to traditional leadership structures. Whereas the American Revolution sought independence from an external power, the French Revolution aimed to completely dismantle the existing social and political order within France. The revolutionaries sought to replace the absolute monarchy of Louis XVI with a government based on the principles of liberty, equality, and fraternity.[4]

The Declaration of the Rights of Man and of the Citizen

The French Revolution produced the Declaration of the Rights of Man and of the Citizen in 1789, a foundational document that asserted the universal rights of individuals and the principle that sovereignty resides with the people.[5] This declaration was a direct challenge to the divine right of kings and the hierarchical structures that had dominated French society for centuries. It redefined leadership as a role grounded in the protection of citizens' rights and the pursuit of the common good.

Napoleon Bonaparte – Leadership Through Conquest

However, the French Revolution also demonstrated the complexities and dangers of radical change. The initial revolutionary fervor eventually gave way to the rise of Napoleon Bonaparte, who used military success and popular support to consolidate power and declare himself Emperor of the French in 1804.[6] Napoleon's leadership was marked by a blend of revolutionary ideals and authoritarian control, demonstrating how the promises of revolutionary change can sometimes be subverted by the allure of power. While Napoleon expanded the principles of the revolution across Europe through conquest, his rule also underscored the fragility of democratic institutions in the face of charismatic authority.

The Latin American Revolutions – Leadership in the Struggle for Independence

The wave of revolutions in Latin America during the early 19th century was inspired by the American and French revolutions and led by figures such as Simón Bolívar, José de San Martín, and Miguel Hidalgo. These leaders sought to overthrow European colonial rule and establish independent republics based on the principles of equality and self-determination.[7]

Simón Bolívar – The Liberator

Simón Bolívar, known as "El Libertador," was one of the most prominent leaders in the Latin American struggle for independence. Bolívar's vision extended beyond mere independence; he sought to unite the newly liberated territories into a single, federated republic that could stand as a beacon of republicanism in the Americas.[8] However, Bolívar's leadership also reflected the challenges of maintaining unity and democracy in the aftermath of revolution. Despite his successes, the newly independent states soon fractured into smaller nations, each with its own struggles to establish stable governance.

The Challenges of Post-Revolutionary Leadership

The Latin American revolutions highlighted the difficulties of translating revolutionary ideals into lasting political structures. The new republics faced significant challenges, including economic instability, social divisions, and external pressures. Leaders who had been instrumental in the fight for independence often found it difficult to transition from military command to civilian leadership, leading to a cycle of political turmoil and authoritarian rule in many countries.[2] These challenges underscore the complexities of leadership in the aftermath of revolution and the ongoing struggle to build institutions that reflect democratic values.

The Enduring Legacy of Revolutionary Leadership

The revolutions of the late 18th and early 19th centuries fundamentally transformed the nature of leadership and authority. They established new norms of governance based on the consent of the governed, the protection of individual rights, and the idea that leadership should serve the common good rather than the interests of a ruling elite. These revolutions also highlighted the challenges of maintaining democratic principles in the face of power struggles, economic pressures, and social divisions.

The legacy of revolutionary leadership continues to influence modern political thought and practice. The principles of equality, representation, and the rule of law, which were championed by the revolutionaries, remain central to contemporary discussions about leadership and governance. At the same time, the revolutions remind us of the fragility of democratic institutions and the need for constant vigilance to ensure that leadership remains accountable to the people.

Conclusion

Leadership in the Age of Revolutions marked a dramatic shift away from monarchic and authoritarian models of governance. The revolutionary leaders of this period redefined what it meant to be a leader, emphasizing the importance of consent, accountability, and the protection of individual rights. As we continue to explore the evolution of leadership in this book, it is essential to consider how the lessons of these revolutions can inform our current approaches to leadership and help us navigate the challenges of modern governance.

Discussion Questions

1.   How did the American and French revolutions challenge traditional notions of leadership and authority? What new principles of leadership emerged from these revolutions?

2.   Reflect on how these revolutions redefined leadership in terms of popular sovereignty, equality, and individual rights. How do these principles continue to influence modern governance?

3.   George Washington is often celebrated as a model of democratic leadership. What aspects of Washington's leadership set him apart from traditional monarchs, and how did his actions shape the future of American governance?

4.   Discuss Washington's decision to relinquish power and how this set a precedent for peaceful transitions of power and the principle of temporary, accountable leadership.

5.   The French Revolution produced both democratic ideals and the rise of Napoleon Bonaparte. How does Napoleon's leadership illustrate the complexities of revolutionary change?

6.   Explore the tension between revolutionary ideals and the consolidation of power in the figure of Napoleon. How did his leadership both advance and undermine the goals of the revolution?

7.   Simón Bolívar sought to create a unified republic in Latin America. What challenges did Bolívar and other Latin American leaders face in translating revolutionary ideals into stable governance?

8.   Consider the difficulties of post-revolutionary leadership in Latin America. How did the challenges of unity, economic instability, and social divisions impact the success of these new republics?

9.   The Age of Revolutions introduced the idea that leadership should be accountable to the people. How can modern

leaders uphold this principle in the face of contemporary challenges such as political polarization and economic inequality?

10.   Discuss the ongoing relevance of revolutionary leadership principles in today's political landscape. What strategies can leaders use to maintain accountability and serve the common good?

11.   What lessons can be learned from the successes and failures of revolutionary leaders in establishing democratic institutions? How can these lessons inform current efforts to promote democracy and good governance?

12.   Reflect on the importance of building strong institutions that can sustain democratic values over time. How can the experiences of past revolutions guide current and future efforts to strengthen democratic governance?

CHAPTER SIX:

The Modern Leadership Enterprise – A New Era of Corporate Leadership

Introduction

The modern era has witnessed the emergence of a new form of leadership—one that is heavily influenced by the corporate world. Leadership has evolved into a professional enterprise, with a strong emphasis on management theories, organizational efficiency, and measurable outcomes. This chapter explores how corporate leadership has shaped the contemporary understanding of what it means to lead, examining both the benefits and challenges of this model through the lens of biblical principles.

The Rise of Corporate Leadership

In the 20th and 21st centuries, leadership became increasingly associated with the corporate sector. The expansion of global markets, the rise of multinational corporations, and the development of complex organizational structures all contributed to the professionalization of leadership. Leadership, once viewed as a calling or a public service, began to be seen as a skill set that could be learned, taught, and applied across various industries.[1]

The development of business schools, leadership training programs, and a booming self-help industry reflected this shift.

Leadership became commodified, with a focus on strategies, techniques, and personal development. The goal was often to maximize efficiency, profitability, and growth, which led to the creation of leadership models that emphasized results over relationships and bottom-line success over ethical consider- ations.[2]

This shift in focus is reminiscent of the warning in James 4:13- 14, where the author cautions against arrogance in planning and the pursuit of worldly success: "Now listen, you who say, 'Today or tomorrow we will go to this or that city, spend a year there, carry on business and make money.' Why, you do not even know what will happen tomorrow. What is your life? You are a mist that appears for a little while and then vanishes."[3] The pursuit of corporate success can often lead to a neglect of deeper values and a misunderstanding of the true purpose of leadership.

The Professionalization of Leadership

The professionalization of leadership has brought both positive and negative consequences. On the one hand, it has led to the development of sophisticated tools and methods for managing large organizations. Leadership has become more intentional, with clear goals, metrics, and strategies designed to achieve success.[4] On the other hand, this approach has also led to a reductionist view of leadership, where the focus is primarily on efficiency and outcomes, often at the expense of people and relationships.[5]

In many ways, this professionalized approach contrasts sharply with the biblical view of leadership, which emphasizes serv- anthood, humility, and the well-being of others. Jesus taught that true leadership is about serving others rather than seeking personal gain or recognition. In Mark 10:42-45, He says, "You know that those who are regarded as rulers of the Gentiles lord it over them, and their high officials exercise authority over them. Not so with you. Instead, whoever wants to be- come great among you must be your servant, and whoever wants to be first must be slave of all. For even the Son of Man did not come to be served, but to serve, and to give His life as a ransom for many."[6]

This passage highlights the contrast between worldly leadership, which often seeks power and control, and godly leadership, which seeks to serve and uplift others. The professionalization of leadership can sometimes obscure this essential truth, leading to a model of leadership that prioritizes success over service.[7]

Leadership as a Commodity

The commodification of leadership has also led to the rise of the leadership industry—a multibillion-dollar enterprise that includes leadership books, seminars, coaching, and consulting services. While there is value in learning and growing as a leader, the commercialization of leadership raises important questions about motivation and purpose.[8]

In a marketplace-driven approach, there is a risk that leadership becomes more about personal advancement, fame, or financial gain than about genuine service and stewardship. This temptation is addressed in 1 Timothy 6:10, which warns, "For the love of money is a root of all kinds of evil. Some people, eager for money, have wandered from the faith and pierced themselves with many griefs."[9] When leadership is driven by the pursuit of wealth or status, it can lead to moral and ethical compromises that ultimately undermine the integrity and effectiveness of leadership.

Moreover, the focus on self-help and personal success can sometimes overshadow the communal and relational aspects of leadership that are so central to the biblical narrative. Leadership, in a Christian context, is not just about individual achievement but about guiding and serving a community in a way that honors God and reflects His love and justice.[10]

The Biblical Call to Stewardship

Despite the challenges posed by the modern leadership enterprise, there are also opportunities to reclaim a biblical vision of leadership within this context. One of the key biblical principles that can inform modern corporate leadership is the concept of stewardship. In the Bible, stewardship refers to the responsible management of the resources, people, and opportunities that God has entrusted to us.

This idea is powerfully expressed in the Parable of the Talents (Matthew 25:14-30), where Jesus tells the story of a master who entrusts his servants with various amounts of money (talents) and expects them to invest and manage these resources wisely. The servant who faithfully invests and multiplies his talents is commended, while the one who hides his talent out of fear is condemned.[11]

The parable highlights the importance of using our gifts, talents, and resources wisely and faithfully. In a corporate context, this means that leaders are called to steward the resources of their organizations in a way that honors God, benefits others, and contributes to the common good. This includes making decisions that are ethical, just, and aligned with biblical values, even when doing so may not maximize profits or lead to immediate success.[12]

Furthermore, biblical stewardship emphasizes accountability. Leaders are accountable to God for how they use the authority and resources entrusted to them. This accountability is a sobering reminder that leadership is not about personal gain but about serving others and fulfilling God's purposes.[13]

Servant Leadership in the Corporate World

The modern corporate world presents both challenges and opportunities for applying biblical principles of leadership. While the focus on efficiency, productivity, and profitability can sometimes conflict with the biblical call to serve and care for others, there are also many ways in which Christian leaders can bring a positive influence to their organizations.

Servant leadership, as modeled by Jesus, is a powerful framework for transforming corporate leadership. This approach emphasizes humility, empathy, and a commitment to the well-being of others. In Philippians 2:3-4, Paul writes, "Do nothing out of selfish ambition or vain conceit. Rather, in humility value others above yourselves, not looking to your own interests but each of you to the interests of the others."[14] This passage provides a blueprint for how leaders can approach their roles in the corporate world—not as lords over their subordinates, but as servants who seek the best for their teams, clients, and communities.

Servant leadership in a corporate context might involve prioritizing the development and well-being of employees, making ethical decisions that benefit society, or fostering a corporate culture that values integrity, transparency, and compassion. It is about seeing leadership not as a means to an end but as an opportunity to reflect God's character and advance His kingdom through the work that we do.[15]

Conclusion: Reclaiming a Biblical Vision for Leadership

The modern leadership enterprise, with its emphasis on professionalism, efficiency, and success, offers many tools and insights that can enhance the practice of leadership. However, it also presents significant challenges that require a careful and critical approach. As Christians, we are called to reclaim a biblical vision for leadership—one that prioritizes service, stewardship, and accountability to God.

By integrating the principles of servant leadership, stewardship, and humility into the corporate world, Christian leaders can model a different way of leading—one that reflects the values of the Kingdom of God rather than the values of the marketplace.

In doing so, they can transform their organizations and their communities, bringing light into the darkness and hope into a world that desperately needs it.

Discussion Questions

1.   How has the professionalization of leadership in the corporate world both benefited and challenged the practice of leadership from a biblical perspective? What are the key differences between corporate leadership models and biblical leadership principles?

2.   Mark 10:42-45 presents Jesus's model of servant leadership. How can this model be applied in the corporate world, where the focus is often on efficiency and profit? What are the potential challenges and rewards of adopting a servant leadership approach in business?

3.   Reflect on the commodification of leadership and the rise of the leadership industry. How does 1 Timothy 6:10's warning about the love of money apply to modern leadership practices? How can leaders ensure their motivations remain pure and aligned with biblical values?

4.   The Parable of the Talents (Matthew 25:14-30) emphasizes the importance of stewardship. How can corporate leaders practice stewardship in their roles? What does it mean to be accountable to God in a business context?

5.   Philippians 2:3-4 speaks of valuing others above oneself. How can this principle be integrated into corporate leadership practices? What impact might this have on workplace culture and employee well-being?

6.   Discuss the concept of accountability in leadership, particularly in the context of the modern corporate world. How can leaders balance the demands of profitability with the need to maintain ethical and moral integrity?

CHAPTER SEVEN:

The Crisis of Leadership – Failures, Corruption, and Disillusionment

Introduction

In recent decades, the world has witnessed numerous leadership failures across various sectors—political, corporate, and even religious. These failures have not only caused significant harm but have also led to widespread disillusionment with the very concept of leadership. As leaders fall from grace due to scandals, corruption, and moral failures, the trust that people once placed in their leaders has been severely eroded. This chapter explores the causes and consequences of this crisis in leadership and reflects on how biblical principles can guide us in addressing these challenges.

The Crisis in Political Leadership

Political leadership has always been fraught with challenges, but in recent years, the scale of corruption, abuse of power, and moral failures among leaders has reached alarming levels. From embezzlement and bribery to the manipulation of power for personal gain, political scandals have become all too common. These failures have not only undermined the credibility of individual leaders but have also damaged the institutions they represent.

The Bible provides numerous examples of political leaders who fell into corruption and how their actions led to dire consequences for themselves and their nations. One such example is King Saul, whose disobedience to God led to his downfall. In 1 Samuel 15:22-23, the prophet Samuel rebukes Saul, saying, "Does the Lord delight in burnt offerings and sacrifices as much as in obeying the Lord? To obey is better than sacrifice, and to heed is better than the fat of rams. For rebellion is like the sin of divination, and arrogance like the evil of idolatry. Because you have rejected the word of the Lord, He has rejected you as king."[1]

Saul's failure to obey God's commands led to his rejection as king, illustrating the consequences of a leader's moral failure. Similarly, the ongoing crises in political leadership today often stem from a disregard for ethical and moral standards, resulting in a loss of public trust and the destabilization of governance.[2]

Corporate Leadership Failures

The corporate world has also seen its share of leadership crises, with high-profile cases of fraud, unethical business practices, and the exploitation of workers and resources for profit. The collapse of companies like Enron and the financial crisis of 2008 serve as stark reminders of what can happen when corporate leaders prioritize personal gain over ethical responsibility.[3]

These corporate scandals have far-reaching consequences, including job losses, financial ruin for countless individuals, and a deepening sense of distrust in corporate institutions. James 5:1-6 speaks to the dangers of wealth obtained through injustice, warning, "Now listen, you rich people, weep and wail because of the misery that is coming on you. Your wealth has rotted, and moths have eaten your clothes. Your gold and silver are corroded. Their corrosion will testify against you and eat your flesh like fire. You have hoarded wealth in the last days. Look! The wages you failed to pay the workers who mowed your fields are crying out against you. The cries of the harvesters have reached the ears of the Lord Almighty."[4]

This passage highlights the importance of justice and fairness in the accumulation of wealth and power. Corporate leaders who ignore these principles in favor of greed and exploitation ultimately face judgment, both in the eyes of the public and, as Scripture suggests, in the eyes of God.[5]

Failures in Religious Leadership

Perhaps the most disheartening leadership failures occur within religious institutions, where leaders are expected to uphold the highest moral and ethical standards. Unfortunately, religious leaders are not immune to corruption, scandal, and moral failure. High-profile cases of sexual abuse, financial misconduct, and the abuse of power within churches and religious organizations have shaken the faith of many and led to widespread disillusionment.[6]

The Bible is clear about the responsibilities of spiritual leaders and the consequences of their failures. In Ezekiel 34:2-4, God speaks through the prophet against the leaders of Israel, saying, "Woe to you shepherds of Israel who only take care of yourselves! Should not shepherds take care of the flock? You eat the curds, clothe yourselves with the wool and slaughter the choice animals, but you do not take care of the flock. You have not strengthened the weak or healed the sick or bound up the injured. You have not brought back the strays or searched for the lost. You have ruled them harshly and brutally."[7]

This rebuke is a powerful reminder that religious leaders are called to serve their communities with humility, compassion, and integrity. When they fail in these duties, the damage is profound, not only to their own reputations but to the faith and trust of those they lead.[8]

The Consequences of Leadership Failures

The consequences of leadership failures are far-reaching. When leaders fail, the ripple effects can be felt across entire organizations, communities, and even nations. Trust is eroded, morale declines, and the sense of collective purpose is weakened. In many cases, these failures lead to a crisis of legitimacy, where people no longer believe in the institutions or the individuals who lead them.

Proverbs 29:2 captures this dynamic well: "When the righteous thrive, the people rejoice; when the wicked rule, the people groan."[2] When leaders act with integrity and righteousness, their communities flourish. But when they fall into corruption and moral failure, the people suffer.

In addition to the social and organizational consequences, leadership failures also have spiritual implications. Leaders are held to a higher standard because of the influence they wield, and when they fall, they not only lead others astray but also dishonor God. James 3:1 warns, "Not many of you should become teachers, my fellow believers, because you know that we who teach will be judged more strictly."[10] This verse emphasizes the weight of responsibility that comes with leadership, particularly within the Church.

Responding to the Crisis

In the face of widespread leadership failures, how should we respond? The Bible offers several principles that can guide us in navigating these challenging times.

1.   Repentance and Accountability

The first step in addressing leadership failures is repentance. Leaders who have fallen must acknowledge their wrongdoing, seek forgiveness, and take steps to make amends. This is true not only for individual leaders but also for the institutions they represent. Accountability is essential for restoring trust and integrity. Proverbs 28:13 states, "Whoever conceals their sins does not prosper, but the one who confesses and renounces them finds mercy." Transparency and accountability are key to moving forward after a leadership failure.[11]

2.   Restoration and Reconciliation

After repentance, the process of restoration can begin. This involves not only the personal restoration of the fallen leader but also the restoration of trust within the community. Galatians 6:1 encourages, "Brothers and sisters, if someone is caught in a sin, you who live by the Spirit should restore that person gently. But watch yourselves, or you also may be tempted." Restoration must be handled with care, compassion, and a commitment to justice.[12]

3.   Renewed Commitment to Ethical Leadership

Finally, leadership failures call for a renewed commitment to ethical and moral leadership. Leaders must recommit to the principles of integrity, humility, and service. This involves fostering a culture of accountability and transparency within organizations and encouraging leaders to lead by example, following the model of Christ, who "humbled Himself by becoming obedient to death—even death on a cross!" (Philippians 2:8).[13]

Conclusion: Rebuilding Trust in Leadership

The crisis of leadership that we face today is a call to action. It is an opportunity to reassess our values, recommit to ethical leadership, and rebuild trust in our institutions. By returning to the biblical principles of humility, service, and integrity, we can address the root causes of leadership failures and work towards a future where leaders are once again worthy of the trust and respect of those they lead.

In doing so, we can restore hope in the possibility of righteous leadership—leadership that honors God, serves the people, and brings about flourishing in every sphere of life.

Discussion Questions

1.   Reflect on the example of King Saul in 1 Samuel 15:22-23. How does Saul's failure to obey God serve as a warning for leaders today? What lessons can be learned about the importance of obedience and accountability in leadership?

2.   James 5:1-6 warns against the dangers of wealth obtained through injustice. How can corporate leaders today ensure that their pursuit of success does not come at the expense of ethical integrity and the well-being of others?

3.   Ezekiel 34:2-4 rebukes the shepherds of Israel for failing to care for their flock. How does this passage apply to religious leaders today? What responsibilities do spiritual leaders have to their communities, and how can they avoid the pitfalls of power and corruption?

4.   Proverbs 29:2 contrasts the outcomes of righteous versus wicked leadership. In what ways have recent leadership failures affected your trust in political, corporate, or religious institutions? How can these institutions rebuild trust after a crisis?

5.   Galatians 6:1 speaks of restoring those who have fallen into sin with gentleness. What role does restoration play in addressing leadership failures? How can leaders and communities balance justice and mercy in the process of restoration?

6.   Philippians 2:8 highlights Jesus's humility and obedience. How can leaders today emulate Christ's example in their leadership roles? What practical steps can they take to ensure that their leadership is characterized by humility and service rather than pride and control?

CHAPTER EIGHT:

The Rise of Followership – A Shift Towards Collective Influence

Introduction

For much of history, leadership has been viewed as the driving force behind societal progress, with leaders occupying center stage as the visionaries and decision-makers. However, in recent years, there has been a growing recognition of the importance of followership—the idea that those who follow are as crucial to the success of an organization or movement as those who lead. This chapter explores the rise of followership as a concept, highlighting its importance and examining how it aligns with biblical principles of community, service, and mutual submission.

The Changing Dynamics of Leadership and Followership

Traditionally, leadership has been understood as a top-down process, where a single leader directs, controls, and inspires a group of followers. This model often emphasizes the charisma, authority, and decision-making power of the leader. However, as organizational structures become more complex and society more interconnected, the role of followers has gained increasing importance.

The shift towards recognizing followership stems from the understanding that leadership is not just about the individual at the top but also about the dynamics within the group. Effective leadership requires engaged, committed, and proactive followers who contribute their ideas, skills, and perspectives. In this new paradigm, leadership and followership are seen as interdependent, with both roles contributing to the success of the whole.

This idea is reflected in the biblical concept of the body of Christ, where each member has a role to play. In 1 Corinthians 12:12-14, Paul writes, "Just as a body, though one, has many parts, but all its many parts form one body, so it is with Christ. For we were all baptized by one Spirit so as to form one body—whether Jews or Gentiles, slave or free—and we were all given the one Spirit to drink. Even so the body is not made up of one part but of many."[1] This passage emphasizes that every member of the community, whether in a leadership or followership role, is vital to the functioning of the whole.

The Role of Followership in Biblical Leadership

The Bible provides numerous examples of how followership plays a crucial role in God's plans. From the Israelites following Moses out of Egypt to the disciples following Jesus, the success of God's work often depends on the faithful response of those who follow.

The Israelites and Moses

The story of the Exodus illustrates the importance of followership. Moses, called by God to lead the Israelites out of slavery in Egypt, relied heavily on the cooperation and trust of the people. Despite their fears and doubts, the Israelites followed Moses through the Red Sea and into the wilderness. Their journey was not without challenges, but their willingness to follow Moses was essential to their deliverance.[2]

However, the story also highlights the consequences of poor followership. When the Israelites grumbled against Moses and refused to trust God's plan, they faced severe consequences, including the delay of their entry into the Promised Land (Numbers 14:1-4, 20-23).[3] This narrative underscores the idea that followership is not passive but requires active trust, obedience, and participation in God's work.

The Disciples and Jesus

The New Testament offers perhaps the most profound example of followership in the relationship between Jesus and His disciples. Jesus called His disciples to follow Him, not merely as passive observers, but as active participants in His mission. In Matthew 4:19, Jesus says, "Come, follow Me, and I will send you out to fish for people."[4] This call to follow was an invitation to learn, serve, and eventually lead others in the way of Christ.

The disciples' journey with Jesus was marked by moments of doubt, misunderstanding, and failure. Yet, their commitment to follow Him ultimately led to the spread of the Gospel and the establishment of the early Church. The Great Commission in Matthew 28:19-20, where Jesus instructs His disciples to "go and make disciples of all nations,"[5] is a testament to the impact of their followership. The disciples transitioned from followers to leaders, demonstrating the fluidity between these roles in the context of God's Kingdom.

Mutual Submission and Collective Influence

One of the key biblical principles that undergirds the concept of followership is mutual submission. The idea that we are called to submit to one another out of reverence for Christ is central to Christian community and leadership. In Ephesians 5:21, Paul writes, "Submit to one another out of reverence for Christ."[6] This mutual submission fosters a culture where both leaders and followers are accountable to each other, serving one another in love and humility.

Mutual submission challenges the hierarchical, top-down models of leadership by promoting a more egalitarian approach where influence is shared and leadership is distributed. In such a model, leaders are not above their followers, but alongside them, guiding and serving together. This approach reflects the example of Jesus, who, although He was their teacher and Lord, washed His disciples' feet and commanded them to do the same for others (John 13:12-15).[7]

In practical terms, this means that effective followership involves more than just following orders. It requires critical thinking, active participation, and the willingness to speak up when necessary. It also involves supporting and strengthening the leader, helping to carry the vision forward, and contributing to the collective success of the group.

The Challenges and Opportunities of Followership

While the rise of followership presents many opportunities for enhancing leadership dynamics, it also comes with challenges. One challenge is the cultural perception that followership is a passive or lesser role. In a society that often glorifies leadership, the role of a follower can be undervalued or misunderstood. However, as we have seen, biblical followership is anything but passive; it is a dynamic and active role that requires courage, commitment, and wisdom.

Another challenge is the potential for conflict or power struggles within a group. When followers feel empowered to contribute their ideas and perspectives, there may be times when their views conflict with those of the leader. Navigating these tensions requires humility, open communication, and a shared commitment to the greater good.[8]

Despite these challenges, the rise of followership offers significant opportunities to create more collaborative and effective leadership environments. By recognizing and valuing the contributions of all members of a community or organization, leaders can build stronger, more resilient teams. Moreover, by fostering a culture of mutual submission and collective influence, Christian communities can more fully embody the biblical vision of unity and shared purpose.[9]

Conclusion: Embracing Followership as Part of Leadership

The rise of followership marks a significant shift in how we understand and practice leadership. It reminds us that leadership is not just about those at the top but also about the collective influence of all members of a community or organization. By embracing followership as a vital part of leadership, we can create environments where everyone has a role to play and where leadership is seen as a shared responsibility.

As we seek to follow Christ and lead others, let us remember that effective leadership is rooted in the principles of mutual submission, service, and collective influence. By valuing the contributions of both leaders and followers, we can build communities that reflect the unity, love, and purpose of the body of Christ.

Discussion Questions

1.   Reflect on 1 Corinthians 12:12-14, which describes the body of Christ as having many parts, each with a vital role. How does this passage challenge traditional views of leadership and highlight the importance of followership?

2.   Consider the role of the Israelites in following Moses during the Exodus. What does this story teach us about the responsibilities and challenges of followership? How can we apply these lessons in our own contexts today?

3.   Jesus's relationship with His disciples demonstrates the fluidity between leadership and followership. In what ways can modern followers prepare themselves to take on leadership roles, as the disciples did after Jesus's ascension?

4.   Ephesians 5:21 calls for mutual submission among believers. How can this principle be applied in leadership and followership within a church or organization? What practical steps can be taken to foster a culture of mutual submission?

5.   John 13:12-15 recounts Jesus washing His disciples' feet as an example of servant leadership. How can this example shape the way both leaders and followers interact with each other in a modern organizational context?

6.   Discuss the potential challenges of followership, such as power dynamics and conflict. How can these challenges be addressed in a way that strengthens the community and aligns with biblical principles?

CHAPTER NINE:

The Leadership Principles of Jesus – Servanthood and Humility

Introduction

In a world where leadership is often equated with power, authority, and influence, Jesus offers a radically different model. His approach to leadership is grounded in servanthood, humility, and sacrificial love—principles that challenge conventional paradigms and offer a transformative vision for leadership. This chapter explores how Jesus's leadership principles are demonstrated in His life and teachings, and how they can be practically applied in today's culture.

The Paradox of Servant Leadership

Jesus's approach to leadership turns the world's understanding of power upside down. While many leaders seek to assert their authority and dominate others, Jesus taught that true greatness comes through serving others. In Matthew 20:25-28, He contrasts worldly leadership with the kind of leadership He calls His followers to practice:

"Jesus called them together and said, 'You know that the rulers of the Gentiles lord it over them, and their high officials exercise authority over them. Not so with you. Instead, whoever wants to become great among you must be your servant, and whoever wants to be first must be your slave—just as the Son of Man did not come to be served, but to serve, and to give His life as a ransom for many.'"[1]

This passage highlights the paradox of servant leadership: greatness is found not in being served, but in serving others. In a culture that often associates leadership with prestige, wealth, and control, Jesus's model challenges us to reconsider what it means to lead.

Example: Jesus Washing the Disciples' Feet

One of the most poignant examples of Jesus's servant leadership is found in John 13, where He washes His disciples' feet. Foot-washing in the ancient world was a task reserved for the lowest servants, as it involved cleaning the dusty, dirty feet of those who had traveled on unpaved roads. For Jesus, the Teacher and Lord, to take on this role was both shocking and deeply humbling.

"When He had finished washing their feet, He put on His clothes and returned to His place. 'Do you understand what I have done for you?' He asked them. 'You call me "Teacher" and "Lord," and rightly so, for that is what I am. Now that I, your Lord and Teacher, have washed your feet, you also should wash one another's feet. I have set you an example that you should do as I have done for you'" (John 13:12-15).[2]

Jesus's act of washing His disciples' feet was more than a gesture of humility; it was a powerful demonstration of His leadership philosophy. He was teaching them that true leadership involves serving others, even in the most humble and menial ways.

Application in Today's Culture

In today's culture, where leadership is often about climbing the corporate ladder, seeking recognition, and achieving personal success, Jesus's example of foot-washing challenges us to adopt a different mindset. Servant leadership in the modern world might look like:

◊ Leaders who prioritize the needs of their team members: This could involve taking the time to mentor and develop others, ensuring their growth and success rather than focusing solely on personal advancement.

◊ Executives who practice humility in decision-making: Instead of imposing their will, they actively seek input from others, particularly those who are often overlooked, and are willing to make decisions that benefit the whole organization, even at personal cost.

◊ Public figures who use their platform to serve rather than be served: In a world where celebrity and influence are often used for personal gain, leaders can choose to leverage their influence to advocate for the marginalized, support charitable causes, and serve their communities.

By embracing servant leadership, leaders in today's culture can create environments where people feel valued, empowered, and respected, ultimately leading to more cohesive and effective teams and organizations.[3]

Jesus's Example of Humility

Humility is a central aspect of Jesus's leadership, distinguishing Him from the typical leaders of His time—and ours. Unlike many leaders who seek recognition and honor, Jesus consistently demonstrated humility in His actions and teachings. Paul captures this essence in Philippians 2:5-8, where he calls believers to adopt the same mindset as Christ:

"In your relationships with one another, have the same mindset as Christ Jesus: Who, being in very nature God, did not consider equality with God something to be used to His own advantage; rather, He made Himself nothing by taking the very nature of a servant, being made in human likeness. And being found in appearance as a man, He humbled Himself by becoming obedient to death—even death on a cross!"[4]

Jesus, though fully God, chose to humble Himself by becoming human and submitting to a death that was reserved for the lowest criminals. His humility wasn't just an attitude; it was a way of life that permeated everything He did.

Example: The Incarnation and the Cross

The incarnation itself is a profound act of humility. Jesus, the Creator of the universe, entered into His creation as a helpless infant, born into poverty and obscurity. He lived a life of service, often misunderstood and rejected, ultimately submitting to a humiliating and excruciating death on the cross. This level of humility is unparalleled and serves as the foundation for Christian leadership.[5]

Application in Today's Culture

◊   In a culture that often celebrates self-promotion, ambition, and the pursuit of personal glory, Jesus's example of humility is both countercultural and transformative. Applying this principle today might involve:

◊   Leaders who are willing to admit mistakes: Instead of covering up errors or shifting blame, humble leaders take responsibility for their actions, fostering a culture of transparency and trust.

◊   Executives who resist the lure of power for its own sake: Rather than seeking positions of power to enhance their status, they use their roles to serve others and advance the greater good.

◊   Individuals who choose to elevate others: In competitive environments, humble leaders focus on lifting others up, giving credit where it's due, and celebrating the successes of their team members rather than seeking recognition for themselves.

Incorporating humility into leadership roles helps dismantle toxic power dynamics, creating space for authentic relationships, collaborative decision-making, and a work environment where everyone feels respected and valued.[6]

The Power of Sacrificial Love

At the heart of Jesus's leadership is His sacrificial love, demonstrated most profoundly in His willingness to lay down His life for others. Jesus's leadership was not about exerting power or control but about giving Himself for the sake of others. This sacrificial love is the essence of Christian leadership; it calls leaders to put the needs of others before their own, even when it requires personal sacrifice.

In John 10:11, Jesus declares, "I am the good shepherd. The good shepherd lays down His life for the sheep."[7] This image of the shepherd is a powerful metaphor for leadership: it is protective, nurturing, and self-sacrificing. Jesus didn't just lead His followers; He gave His life for them, demonstrating the ultimate act of love.

Example: The Cross as the Ultimate Sacrifice

The cross is the ultimate symbol of sacrificial love. Jesus, innocent and without sin, willingly endured the agony of crucifixion to redeem humanity. In doing so, He redefined what it means to be a leader: it is not about what one can gain but about what one is willing to give.

Paul reflects on this sacrificial love in Romans 5:8: "But God demonstrates His own love for us in this: While we were still sinners, Christ died for us."[8] Jesus's death on the cross wasn't just an act of love for His followers; it was an act of love for all of humanity, even for those who rejected Him.

Application in Today's Culture

In today's culture, where leadership is often about maximizing personal gain and minimizing personal loss, the principle of sacrificial love challenges leaders to reorient their priorities. Applying sacrificial love in modern leadership might involve:

◊ Leaders who prioritize the well-being of their employees: This could mean making decisions that protect jobs, even if it means lower profits, or creating policies that promote work-life balance, even if it means slower growth.

◊ Public figures who use their influence to advocate for justice and compassion: Rather than seeking popularity, they stand for what is right, even when it is unpopular or comes at a personal cost.

◊ Parents and caregivers who lead with sacrificial love: In the home, this might look like parents who put aside their own desires to invest time, energy, and resources into their children's development and well-being.

By leading with sacrificial love, leaders create environments where trust, loyalty, and genuine care flourish. This approach not only benefits those being led but also transforms the leader, fostering deeper connections and a greater sense of purpose.[2]

The Call to Imitate Christ's Leadership

Jesus's leadership principles—servanthood, humility, and sacrificial love—are not merely ideals to admire; they are a call to action for all who follow Him. Jesus explicitly called His disciples to follow His example, and this call extends to us today. In John 13:34-35, Jesus commands, "A new command I give you: Love one another. As I have loved you, so you must love one another. By this everyone will know that you are My disciples, if you love one another."[10]

This call to imitate Christ's love is at the heart of Christian leadership. It challenges us to lead in ways that reflect Jesus's values and priorities, transforming not only how we lead but also the lives of those we lead.

Challenges in Embracing Jesus's Leadership Model

Embracing Jesus's leadership model is not without its challenges. In a world that often values power, prestige, and self-interest, leading like Jesus requires a deep reliance on God and a willingness to go against the cultural current. Some challenges include:

◊ Resisting the temptation to seek recognition: In a culture that often equates success with visibility and fame, choosing to lead with humility and without seeking the spotlight can be difficult.

◊ Sacrificing personal gain for the benefit of others: Leading with sacrificial love means being willing to give up time, resources, and sometimes personal advancement for the sake of others.

◊ Maintaining integrity in the face of pressure: Whether in business, politics, or ministry, the pressure to compromise on ethical standards can be immense. Leading like Jesus requires a steadfast commitment to righteousness, even when it is costly.

The Transformative Impact of Jesus's Leadership

Despite these challenges, embracing Jesus's leadership principles can have a profound impact. When leaders choose to serve rather than be served, to act with humility rather than pride, and to love sacrificially rather than selfishly, they create environments where people feel valued, supported, and empowered. This kind of leadership reflects the heart of God and has the potential to transform not only the leader but also those who are led.

As we strive to lead like Jesus, we participate in His redemptive work, bringing light to dark places and hope to those who are lost. The leadership principles of Jesus are not just a path to personal fulfillment; they are a call to contribute to the advancement of God's Kingdom on earth.

Conclusion: Leading Like Jesus

The leadership principles of Jesus—servanthood, humility, and sacrificial love—offer a radically different approach to leadership than what the world typically values. By following Jesus's example, we can become leaders who not only achieve success but also bring about lasting change that honors God and blesses others.

As we reflect on Jesus's model of leadership, let us be challenged to embrace these principles in our own lives and leadership roles. May we lead with the heart of a servant, the humility of a follower, and the love of a shepherd, always looking to Jesus as our ultimate example.

Discussion Questions

1.   Reflect on Jesus's act of washing His disciples' feet in John 13:12-15. How does this example challenge our modern views of leadership, and what are practical ways we can serve others in our leadership roles today?

2.   In Philippians 2:5-8, Paul describes Jesus's humility in becoming human and obedient to death. How can this example of humility be applied in leadership positions where pride and ambition are often rewarded?

3.   Consider the concept of sacrificial love as demonstrated by Jesus in John 10:11 and Romans 5:8. What are some ways leaders today can embody sacrificial love in their decision-making and interactions with others?

4.   Jesus calls us to love one another as He has loved us (John 13:34-35). How can this command shape our leadership practices in both personal and professional contexts?

5.   Discuss the challenges of embracing Jesus's leadership model in a culture that values power and success. What are some strategies for overcoming these challenges and remaining faithful to Jesus's principles?

6.   In what ways can leading like Jesus—through servanthood, humility, and sacrificial love—transform not only the leader but also the community or organization they lead? How can this transformation be encouraged in today's leadership environments?

CHAPTER TEN:

Servant Leadership in a Modern Context –
Redefining Power and Influence

Introduction

In a world where power and influence are often equated with control, dominance, and authority, the concept of servant leadership offers a transformative alternative. Rooted in the teachings and example of Jesus, servant leadership emphasizes humility, service to others, and the ethical use of power. This chapter explores how servant leadership can be applied in modern contexts, redefining traditional notions of leadership and offering a more inclusive, compassionate, and effective approach to leading others.

The Core Principles of Servant Leadership

Servant leadership is based on the idea that the primary role of a leader is to serve others. This concept, while countercultural in many ways, is deeply embedded in the teachings of Jesus. In Mark 10:42-45, Jesus contrasts the leadership of the world with the leadership He calls His followers to embody:

"Jesus called them together and said, 'You know that those who are regarded as rulers of the Gentiles lord it over them, and their high officials exercise authority over them. Not so with you. Instead, whoever wants to become great among you must be your servant, and whoever wants to be first must be slave of all. For even the Son of Man did not come to be served, but to serve, and to give His life as a ransom for many.'"[1]

This passage encapsulates the essence of servant leadership: greatness in the Kingdom of God is not measured by how much power one wields, but by how well one serves others. The leader's role is to uplift, empower, and care for those they lead, rather than to dominate or control.

Application in Modern Leadership

In today's leadership environments—whether in business, politics, education, or ministry—servant leadership challenges the traditional hierarchy and offers a more relational and ethical approach to leading. Modern applications of servant leadership might include:

◊ Empowering Team Members: A servant leader focuses on developing the potential of others, helping them grow and succeed. This could involve mentoring, providing opportunities for professional development, and encouraging collaboration.

◊ Prioritizing Ethical Decision-Making: In a world where success is often measured by profits or power, servant leaders prioritize making decisions that are ethically sound and beneficial for the well-being of all stakeholders, even if it means sacrificing short-term gains.

◊ Creating Inclusive Environments: Servant leadership involves creating spaces where everyone's voice is heard and valued. This could mean fostering diversity and inclusion in the workplace, ensuring that all team members feel respected and have the opportunity to contribute.[2]

Redefining Power and Influence

One of the most significant ways servant leadership redefines traditional leadership is by transforming the understanding of power and influence. In many leadership models, power is seen as something to be exercised over others—an instrument of control. However, in servant leadership, power is viewed as a tool for empowering others and enabling them to thrive.

Example: Jesus and the Centurion

The story of Jesus and the centurion in Matthew 8:5-13 illustrates this redefinition of power. The centurion, a Roman officer with considerable authority, approaches Jesus to ask for healing for his servant. Despite his position of power, the centurion displays humility and recognizes Jesus's authority:

"The centurion replied, 'Lord, I do not deserve to have you come under my roof. But just say the word, and my servant will be healed. For I myself am a man under authority, with soldiers under me. I tell this one, "Go," and he goes; and that one, "Come," and he comes. I say to my servant, "Do this," and he does it.' When Jesus heard this, He was amazed and said to those following Him, 'Truly I tell you, I have not found anyone in Israel with such great faith.'"[3]

The centurion's understanding of authority and power was not about exerting control, but about recognizing the power of Jesus's word and submitting to it. This story demonstrates that true power in leadership comes from faith, humility, and a recognition of the greater authority of God.

Application in Modern Leadership

In a modern context, this redefinition of power might look like:

◊   Leading with Humility: Leaders who recognize that their power is not an end in itself but a means to serve others are more likely to lead with humility. This might involve being open to feedback, admitting mistakes, and showing a willingness to learn from others, regardless of their position.

◊   Influencing Through Service: Instead of using influence to manipulate or control outcomes, servant leaders use their

influence to serve the greater good. This could mean advocating for policies or practices that benefit the wider community, supporting initiatives that promote social justice, or
using one's platform to amplify marginalized voices.

◊   Building Trust and Loyalty: Servant leadership builds
trust and loyalty among followers, as people are more likely
to follow a leader who genuinely cares for their well-being
and acts with integrity. This kind of influence is enduring
and fosters a sense of community and shared purpose.[4]

The Challenges of Servant Leadership in a Competitive World

While the principles of servant leadership are powerful and
transformative, they can also be challenging to implement in a
world that often values competition, efficiency, and personal
advancement over collaboration, compassion, and selflessness.

Example: Jesus' Temptation in the Wilderness

The challenges of servant leadership can be likened to the
temptations Jesus faced in the wilderness, as recorded in Matthew 4:1-11. After fasting for forty days, Jesus is tempted by
Satan to use His power for personal gain—to turn stones into
bread, to throw Himself from the temple to test God's protection, and to gain all the kingdoms of the world in exchange for
worshiping Satan.

> *"Jesus said to him, 'Away from me, Satan! For it is written:
> "Worship the Lord your God, and serve Him only."' Then the
> devil left Him, and angels came and attended Him" (Matthew
> 4:10-11).*[5]

Jesus' rejection of these temptations reflects the essence of
servant leadership: the refusal to use power for self-serving
purposes and the commitment to serve God and others above
all else.

Application in Modern Leadership

In today's competitive environments, leaders may face similar temptations to prioritize personal success, wealth, or recognition over the well-being of others. The challenges of implementing servant leadership might include:

◊ Resisting the Temptation to Compromise Ethics: In a world where cutting corners and making compromises can often lead to quicker success, servant leaders must be steadfast in their commitment to ethical principles, even when it's difficult or costly.

◊ Balancing Profit with Purpose: For business leaders, the pressure to prioritize profit can be intense. Servant leaders are called to balance the pursuit of profit with a commitment to social responsibility, ensuring that their decisions benefit not just shareholders but also employees, customers, and the community.

◊ Overcoming Cynicism and Resistance: In some organizational cultures, the principles of servant leadership may be met with skepticism or resistance. Leaders who choose this path must be prepared to face challenges and pushback, remaining committed to their values even when they are not popular.[6]

The Transformative Potential of Servant Leadership

Despite the challenges, servant leadership has the potential to bring about profound and positive change in organizations, communities, and society at large. By redefining power as a tool for service rather than control, and by leading with humility and compassion, servant leaders can create environments where people are empowered, respected, and valued.

Example: The Early Church

The early Church provides a powerful example of the transformative potential of servant leadership. In Acts 2:42-47, we see a community of believers who embodied the principles of servant leadership, sharing their resources, caring for one another, and serving the needs of their community:

"They devoted themselves to the apostles' teaching and to fellowship, to the breaking of bread and to prayer. Everyone was filled with awe at the many wonders and signs performed by the apostles. All the believers were together and had everything in common. They sold property and possessions to give to anyone who had need. Every day they continued to meet together in the temple courts. They broke bread in their homes and ate together with glad and sincere hearts, praising God and enjoying the favor of all the people. And the Lord added to their number daily those who were being saved."[z]

This passage illustrates the power of a community led by servant leadership. The early Church's commitment to serving one another and their broader community not only strengthened their internal bonds but also attracted others to the faith, leading to the growth of the Church.

Application in Modern Leadership

In modern contexts, the transformative potential of servant leadership might be realized through:

◊   Creating Collaborative Cultures: Servant leaders foster cultures where collaboration, rather than competition, is valued. This could involve encouraging cross-departmental teamwork, recognizing and rewarding collaborative efforts, and creating spaces where everyone's contributions are valued.

◊   Promoting Social Responsibility: In business and government, servant leaders advocate for policies and practices that prioritize the common good. This might include supporting sustainable practices, advocating for fair wages, or leading initiatives that address social inequalities.

◊   Building Inclusive Communities: Servant leaders are committed to creating inclusive environments where everyone, regardless of background or status, is welcomed and valued. This can lead to more diverse, equitable, and thriving organizations and communities.[8]

Conclusion: The Future of Leadership Through Service

As the world continues to evolve, the need for a new model of leadership—one that is grounded in service, humility, and ethical responsibility—becomes increasingly clear. Servant leadership offers a powerful and transformative approach that redefines power and influence, focusing on the well-being and growth of others.

By embracing the principles of servant leadership, leaders can create environments where people are empowered, communities are strengthened, and organizations thrive. In doing so, they not only achieve success but also contribute to a more just, compassionate, and equitable world.

As we look to the future, let us be inspired by the example of Jesus, the ultimate servant leader, and commit ourselves to leading in ways that honor God, serve others, and bring about positive change in the world.

Discussion Questions

1.	Reflect on Mark 10:42-45, where Jesus teaches about servant leadership. How does this passage challenge traditional notions of power and influence, and what practical steps can leaders take to embody this model in their own roles?

2.	The story of Jesus and the centurion in Matthew 8:5-13 highlights the centurion's understanding of authority and power. How can modern leaders apply the centurion's humility and recognition of greater authority in their leadership practices?

3.	In what ways can the challenges faced by Jesus during His temptation in the wilderness (Matthew 4:1-11) relate to the temptations that modern leaders might face? How can leaders resist these temptations and stay true to the principles of servant leadership?

4.	Consider the example of the early Church in Acts 2:42-47. How did their commitment to servant leadership impact their community and contribute to the growth of the Church? How can modern organizations apply these principles to foster similar growth and community impact?

5.	What are some of the challenges servant leaders might face in today's competitive and profit-driven environments? How can they overcome these challenges while remaining faithful to the principles of servant leadership?

6.	Discuss the potential transformative impact of servant leadership on organizations and communities. What are some specific ways that servant leadership can lead to positive change in today's world?

CHAPTER ELEVEN:

The Future of Leadership – Embracing a New Paradigm

Introduction

Throughout this book, we have explored the evolution of leadership from ancient times to the present, examining how leadership has been understood, practiced, and challenged across different eras. From the divine mandate of kings to the rise of democratic leadership, from the professionalization of leadership in the corporate world to the growing recognition of followership, we have seen that leadership is a dynamic and multifaceted concept. At the heart of this journey has been the exploration of the leadership principles modeled by Jesus— principles that challenge conventional notions of power and offer a transformative vision for the future.

As we conclude, this chapter reflects on the key themes discussed and looks ahead to the future of leadership. How can the principles of servanthood, humility, and collective influence shape the leaders of tomorrow? What might leadership look like if these principles were fully embraced and integrated into our institutions, communities, and organizations? This chapter offers a vision for a new paradigm of leadership—one that is not only effective but also deeply aligned with the values of the Kingdom of God.

Recapping Key Themes: Servanthood, Humility, and Collective Influence

The principles of servant leadership, humility, and collective influence have been central to the discussions in this book. These principles, as modeled by Jesus, offer a compelling alternative to traditional leadership models that often prioritize power, control, and self-interest.

Servanthood: Leading by Serving Others

Jesus' leadership was defined by His commitment to serving others. In Matthew 20:28, Jesus states, "The Son of Man did not come to be served, but to serve, and to give His life as a ransom for many."[1] This principle of servanthood challenges leaders to prioritize the needs of others above their own, to lead with a heart of compassion, and to use their influence to uplift and empower those they lead.

In today's context, embracing servanthood as a core leadership principle might involve leaders in business, politics, and other sectors adopting practices that prioritize the well-being of their employees, constituents, and communities. It could mean fostering a culture of service within organizations, where success is measured not only by profits or power but by the positive impact on people's lives.[2]

Humility: Leading with Humility and Integrity

Humility is another key aspect of Jesus' leadership. In Philippians 2:5-8, Paul calls believers to have the same mindset as Christ, who "made Himself nothing by taking the very nature of a servant" and "humbled Himself by becoming obedient to death—even death on a cross."[3] Jesus' humility was not just about lowering Himself but about being obedient to God's will and serving others, even at great personal cost.

For modern leaders, humility involves recognizing their limitations, being open to learning from others, and leading with integrity. It requires leaders to put aside their egos and focus on the greater good. In practice, this might look like leaders who are willing to admit their mistakes, seek input from those they lead, and make decisions that reflect ethical values rather than personal gain.[4]

Collective Influence: The Power of Followership and Mutual Submission

The rise of followership as a concept has highlighted the importance of collective influence in leadership. In Ephesians 5:21, Paul writes, "Submit to one another out of reverence for Christ."[5] This principle of mutual submission challenges hierarchical models of leadership and promotes a more collaborative and inclusive approach.

Collective influence recognizes that leadership is not the sole responsibility of those at the top but is shared among all members of a community or organization. It values the contributions of every individual and encourages a culture where everyone is empowered to lead in their own way. In today's world, this might involve leaders creating environments where diverse voices are heard and valued, where decisions are made collaboratively, and where everyone is encouraged to take ownership of their role in the organization's success.[6]

Embracing a New Paradigm of Leadership

As we look to the future, the need for a new paradigm of leadership becomes increasingly clear. The challenges facing our world—whether they be economic, social, or environmental—require leaders who are not only capable and competent but also compassionate, humble, and committed to serving others. This new paradigm of leadership, grounded in the principles of servanthood, humility, and collective influence, offers a path forward that is both effective and ethical.

Example: The Leadership of Jesus as a Model for the Future

Jesus' leadership provides a timeless model for the future. His approach to leadership was not about asserting dominance or seeking power but about serving others, leading with integrity, and empowering His followers to continue His work. In John 13:14-15, after washing His disciples' feet, Jesus says, "Now that I, your Lord and Teacher, have washed your feet, you also should wash one another's feet. I have set you an example that you should do as I have done for you."[z]

This example of servant leadership is not only relevant for the church but for all areas of life. Imagine a world where leaders in every sector—government, business, education, and beyond—embrace the principles of Jesus' leadership. Such leaders would prioritize the needs of the marginalized, make decisions that reflect ethical and moral values, and foster environments where everyone is valued and empowered to contribute.[8]

Vision for the Future: Transforming Leadership in Every Sphere

The future of leadership, if shaped by these principles, could lead to profound changes in how organizations and societies function. Some potential outcomes might include:

◊   More Inclusive Organizations: Leadership that values collective influence and mutual submission can lead to more inclusive workplaces, where diversity is celebrated and everyone's contributions are valued. This could result in more innovative and resilient organizations, better equipped to navigate the complexities of the modern world.

◊   Ethical Decision-Making: Leaders who prioritize humility and servanthood are more likely to make decisions that are ethical and just. This could lead to a shift in how success is measured, with a greater emphasis on social responsibility, sustainability, and the common good.

◊ Empowered Communities: When leaders focus on serving and empowering others, communities become stronger and more resilient. This could lead to a greater sense of social cohesion, with individuals and groups working together to address common challenges and build a better future.[2]

Challenges and Opportunities in Embracing a New Paradigm

While the vision of a new paradigm of leadership is inspiring, it is not without challenges. Implementing these principles in a world that often values power, control, and self-interest will require courage, commitment, and a willingness to go against the cultural grain. Leaders who choose this path may face resistance, skepticism, and even opposition.

However, the opportunities are immense. By embracing servant leadership, humility, and collective influence, leaders have the potential to transform not only their organizations but also the broader society. They can create spaces where people are empowered to lead, where ethical decisions guide actions, and where the well-being of others is prioritized above personal gain.[10]

Example: Nehemiah's Leadership in Rebuilding Jerusalem

A powerful biblical example of a leader who embodied these principles is Nehemiah. Faced with the monumental task of rebuilding the walls of Jerusalem, Nehemiah demonstrated servant leadership, humility, and a commitment to collective action. In Nehemiah 2:17-18, he rallies the people by saying, "You see the trouble we are in: Jerusalem lies in ruins, and its gates have been burned with fire. Come, let us rebuild the wall of Jerusalem, and we will no longer be in disgrace." The people responded, "Let us start rebuilding," and together, they accomplished what seemed impossible.[11]

Nehemiah's leadership was characterized by his willingness to serve, his humility in seeking God's guidance, and his ability to mobilize and empower the people to work together. His example offers valuable lessons for modern leaders who seek to embrace this new paradigm.[12]

The Call to Lead Differently

As we conclude, the call to lead differently—to embrace a new paradigm of leadership that is grounded in the values of the Kingdom of God—is clear. This call is not just for those in formal leadership positions but for all of us, as we are all called to influence and serve in our own unique ways.

The principles of servant leadership, humility, and collective influence are not just ideals to aspire to; they are practical, actionable principles that can guide our leadership in every sphere of life. Whether we are leading a large organization, a small team, a community group, or even our families, these principles can help us lead in ways that reflect the heart of God and contribute to the flourishing of others.[13]

Conclusion: A Future Shaped by Servant Leadership

The future of leadership is one that must be shaped by the principles of servanthood, humility, and collective influence. As we look ahead, let us be inspired by the example of Jesus and commit ourselves to leading in ways that honor God, serve others, and bring about positive change in the world.

May we be leaders who are known not for our power or influence, but for our love, humility, and willingness to serve. And as we lead, may we contribute to a future where leadership is not about self-interest or control, but about empowering others, building communities, and advancing the values of the Kingdom of God.

Discussion Questions

1.   Reflect on Matthew 20:28, where Jesus describes His mission as one of service rather than being served. How can this principle of servanthood be integrated into leadership roles today,particularly in contexts where power and authority are highly valued?

2.   Philippians 2:5-8 highlights Jesus' humility and obedience. In what ways can modern leaders practice humility in their decision-making and leadership styles, especially in environments that often reward pride and self-promotion?

3.   Ephesians 5:21 calls for mutual submission among believers. How can the principles of collective influence and shared leadership be applied in organizational settings to create more inclusive and collaborative environments?

4.   Consider Nehemiah's leadership in rebuilding the walls of Jerusalem (Nehemiah 2:17-18). How did his approach embody the principles of servant leadership, humility, and collective influence? What lessons can modern leaders learn from Nehemiah's example?

5.   What are some of the challenges leaders might face when trying to implement the new paradigm of leadership discussed in this chapter? How can they overcome these challenges while staying true to the principles of servant leadership and humility?

6.   Discuss the potential impact of embracing a new paradigm of leadership on society as a whole. How might communities, organizations, and even nations be transformed if leaders across all sectors adopted the principles of servanthood, humility, and collective influence?

CHAPTER TWELVE:

The State of the Church in America – From Discipleship to Celebrity Culture

Introduction

The Church in America has undergone significant changes in recent decades, with many congregations shifting their focus from traditional discipleship to a model increasingly driven by personality, convenience, and consumerism. This shift is evident in the rise of celebrity pastors, worship leaders, and the growing emphasis on attracting large audiences rather than cultivating deep spiritual growth. While this trend has led to growing church attendance and impressive media followings, it has also resulted in a departure from the core mission of the Church: making disciples who follow Jesus and become "fishers of men" (Matthew 4:19).[1]

This chapter explores the current state of the Church in America, examining the implications of this shift and drawing on the insights of leaders like Tim Keller and Alan Hirsch to propose a return to a discipleship-focused model. By rediscovering the biblical call to discipleship, the Church can move beyond the allure of celebrity culture and convenience to fulfill its true mission in the world. Furthermore, a renewed focus on discipleship will lead to a more biblical approach to leadership and followership, creating a church that is more aligned with the teachings of Jesus.

The Rise of Celebrity Culture in the Church

In recent years, the American Church has increasingly mirrored the culture around it, particularly in its embrace of celebrity. Pastors and worship leaders with large followings on social media, bestselling books, and viral sermons have become the faces of modern Christianity. While these leaders often have sincere intentions and impactful ministries, the focus on individual personalities has led to a culture where charisma and public appeal often overshadow spiritual depth and discipleship.[2]

This celebrity-driven model can be seen in the way churches are marketed and structured. Services are often designed to be highly polished and entertaining, with a focus on attracting large crowds rather than fostering deep spiritual growth. The "brand" of a church can sometimes become more important than its mission, and success is often measured by attendance numbers and online engagement rather than by the spiritual maturity of its members.[3]

This trend is reminiscent of Paul's warning in 1 Corinthians 1:12-13, where he rebukes the church for dividing over their allegiance to different leaders: "What I mean is this: One of you says, 'I follow Paul'; another, 'I follow Apollos'; another, 'I follow Cephas'; still another, 'I follow Christ.' Is Christ divided? Was Paul crucified for you? Were you baptized in the name of Paul?"[4] Paul's admonition reminds us that the focus of the Church should always be on Christ, not on human leaders.

The Impact on Discipleship

The shift toward a celebrity-driven model has had a profound impact on discipleship. Discipleship, which Jesus defined as a lifelong process of following Him, learning from Him, and becoming more like Him, has been increasingly reduced to a series of programs or quick-fix solutions. In many churches, discipleship has been rebranded as a "growth track" or a "next steps" program, often consisting of a few weeks of classes designed to help people find their purpose or discover their spiritual gifts.[5]

While these programs can be helpful as an introduction to the Christian faith, they fall short of the deep, transformative process that true discipleship requires. Discipleship is not about completing a course or finding one's purpose; it is about daily taking up one's cross and following Jesus (Luke 9:23). It involves ongoing spiritual formation, accountability, and a commitment to living out the teachings of Christ in every area of life.[6]

Insights from Tim Keller and Alan Hirsch on Discipleship

Tim Keller, in his book **Center Church**, and Alan Hirsch, in his various writings, have both spoken extensively about the importance of discipleship in the life of the Church. Their insights offer a valuable perspective on how the Church in America can return to its true mission.

Tim Keller: Discipleship as a Lifelong Process

Tim Keller emphasizes that discipleship is not just for new believers but for all Christians, throughout their lives. In **Center Church**, Keller argues that true discipleship involves a deep understanding of the gospel and its implications for every aspect of life. He writes, "Discipleship is not just about becoming like Jesus in our character, but also about applying the gospel to every aspect of life—our work, our relationships, our community involvement."[7]

Keller's approach to discipleship is holistic, focusing not only on spiritual practices like prayer and Bible study but also on how the gospel transforms our work, relationships, and engagement with society. He calls for churches to move beyond surface-level teaching and to cultivate environments where believers can grow in their understanding of the gospel and its application to every area of life.

Alan Hirsch: The Missional Church and Discipleship

Alan Hirsch, a leading voice in the missional church movement, argues that discipleship is central to the mission of the Church. In his writings, Hirsch challenges the Church to move away from consumer-driven models of ministry and to embrace a missional approach that prioritizes discipleship and the multiplication of disciples.[8]

Hirsch emphasizes that discipleship is not just about personal spiritual growth but about equipping believers to be sent out into the world to make more disciples. He writes, "The Church does not exist for itself; it exists for the world, and its mission is to make disciples who will make disciples."[9]

Hirsch calls for a return to the early church's model of discipleship, where believers were deeply committed to following Jesus and to being part of a community that lived out the gospel in tangible ways. This involves a shift from seeing church as a place to receive religious goods and services to seeing it as a community where believers are equipped and sent out to live out their faith in the world.[10]

The Convenience Culture and the Decline of Discipleship

Another factor contributing to the decline of true discipleship in the American Church is the rise of convenience culture. In an age where everything is designed to be fast, easy, and accessible, the concept of discipleship—which requires time, commitment, and often sacrifice—can seem outdated or burdensome. Many churches have responded to this cultural shift by offering "shortcuts" to discipleship, such as four-week growth tracks or online courses that promise to help people discover their purpose quickly and conveniently.[11]

While these programs can be a helpful starting point, they often fail to capture the depth and richness of true discipleship. Discipleship is not a one-time event or a quick fix; it is a lifelong journey of becoming more like Christ. It involves daily dying to self, being transformed by the renewing of our minds (Romans 12:2), and following Jesus in every aspect of our lives.[12]

In the Gospels, Jesus never promised that following Him would be easy. In fact, He often spoke of the cost of discipleship. In Luke 14:27, Jesus says, "And whoever does not carry their cross and follow Me cannot be My disciple."[13] True discipleship requires a willingness to endure hardship, to persevere in faith, and to submit every area of life to the lordship of Christ.

Discipleship and Its Impact on Leadership and Follower-ship

A renewed focus on discipleship will not only strengthen the spiritual lives of individual believers but also lead to a more biblical approach to leadership and followership within the Church.

Biblical Leadership Through Discipleship

True discipleship naturally cultivates biblical leadership. When leaders are deeply committed to following Jesus and growing in His likeness, their leadership is characterized by the principles of servanthood, humility, and integrity. Discipleship teaches leaders to lead as Jesus did—not for personal gain or recognition but for the benefit of others and the glory of God.[14]

As discipleship forms leaders, it encourages them to see leadership not as a position of power but as a responsibility to serve. In John 13:14-15, after washing His disciples' feet, Jesus says, "Now that I, your Lord and Teacher, have washed your feet, you also should wash one another's feet. I have set you an example that you should do as I have done for you."[15] Leaders who are shaped by this example will lead with humility, compassion, and a commitment to the well-being of those they serve.

Additionally, discipleship ensures that leaders are grounded in biblical truth and spiritual maturity. This foundation helps them navigate the challenges of leadership with wisdom and integrity, avoiding the pitfalls of pride, corruption, and the pursuit of personal glory. As leaders grow in their discipleship, they become better equipped to shepherd others, guide their congregations, and make decisions that reflect God's will.[16]

Biblical Followership Through Discipleship

Just as discipleship fosters biblical leadership, it also cultivates a healthy and biblical approach to followership. In a culture that often idolizes leaders and encourages passive followership, true discipleship empowers believers to take an active role in their spiritual growth and in the life of the church.

Biblical followership, as shaped by discipleship, involves more than just attending services or following a charismatic leader. It means engaging deeply with the teachings of Jesus, participating in the life of the church community, and holding both oneself and one's leaders accountable to biblical standards. As Ephesians 4:15-16 describes, this kind of followership contributes to the growth and unity of the church: "Instead, speaking the truth in love, we will grow to become in every respect the mature body of Him who is the head, that is, Christ. From Him, the whole body, joined and held together by every supporting ligament, grows and builds itself up in love, as each part does its work."[17]

Discipleship encourages followers to be active participants in the mission of the church, not merely consumers of religious services. It calls them to live out their faith in tangible ways, serving others, sharing the gospel, and contributing to the health and vitality of the church community. This active, engaged followership helps to prevent the cult of personality and ensures that the church remains focused on Christ rather than on individual leaders.[18]

Returning to a Biblical Model of Discipleship

To address the current state of the Church in America, a return to a biblical model of discipleship is essential. This means moving away from personality-driven, convenience-oriented approaches and embracing a model of discipleship that is deeply rooted in the teachings of Jesus and the early church.

Fostering Authentic Community

One of the key elements of biblical discipleship is authentic community. The early church was characterized by its commitment to living life together, sharing resources, and encouraging one another in the faith. Acts 2:42-47 describes the early believers as "devoted to the apostles' teaching and to fellowship, to the breaking of bread and to prayer." They met together daily, shared their possessions, and supported one another in their walk with Christ.[19]

In today's context, fostering authentic community means creating spaces where believers can build deep, meaningful relationships, hold one another accountable, and support each other in their spiritual growth. This might involve small groups, discipleship partnerships, or other forms of communal life that go beyond the Sunday service and create opportunities for genuine connection and growth.[20]

Emphasizing Spiritual Formation

True discipleship requires more than just attending church services or completing a growth track; it involves ongoing spiritual formation. This includes practices such as prayer, Bible study, worship, and fasting as well as the cultivation of virtues like humility, patience, and love. Spiritual formation is about becoming more like Christ in character and action, allowing the Holy Spirit to transform us from the inside out.[21]

Churches can support spiritual formation by offering resources and opportunities for deepening one's faith, such as Bible study groups, retreats, spiritual direction, and mentorship programs. It also involves teaching and modeling a lifestyle of obedience to Christ, where discipleship is not just about learning but about living out the gospel in everyday life.[22]

Equipping Believers for Mission

Finally, returning to a biblical model of discipleship means equipping believers to be sent out into the world to make disciples. As Alan Hirsch emphasizes, the Church exists for the world, and its mission is to make disciples who will make disciples. This requires a shift from a consumer-driven model of church to a missional model, where every believer is seen as a missionary, called to live out their faith in their workplace, community, and beyond.[23]

Churches can equip believers for mission by providing training in evangelism, social justice, and community engagement as well as by encouraging believers to see their daily work and relationships as opportunities to share the gospel. It also means supporting believers in living out their faith in practical ways, such as serving the poor, advocating for justice, and being a witness to Christ's love in their everyday interactions.[24]

Conclusion: The Call to Rediscover Discipleship

The state of the Church in America today reflects a significant departure from the biblical model of discipleship. The rise of celebrity culture, the emphasis on convenience, and the reduction of discipleship to a program or growth track have all contributed to a weakened and shallow understanding of what it means to follow Jesus.

However, there is hope. By rediscovering the principles of biblical discipleship—authentic community, spiritual formation, and missional living—the Church can return to its true mission of making disciples who follow Jesus and become "fishers of men" (Matthew 4:19).[25] This will require a shift away from personality-driven, convenience-oriented models and a renewed commitment to the transformative, lifelong process of discipleship.

Moreover, a renewed focus on discipleship will lead to a more biblical approach to leadership and followership. As believers grow in their discipleship, they will be better equipped to lead with humility, integrity, and a servant's heart and to follow with active engagement and a commitment to the mission of the Church.

As we look to the future, let us be challenged to embrace the call to discipleship in its fullest sense, following Jesus with our whole hearts, living out His teachings in every area of our lives, and making disciples who will do the same.

Discussion Questions

1.   Reflect on 1 Corinthians 1:12-13, where Paul addresses divisions in the church based on allegiance to different leaders. How does this passage speak to the current trend of celebrity culture in the Church, and what steps can be taken to refocus on Christ rather than individual personalities?

2.   In Matthew 4:19, Jesus calls His disciples to follow Him and become "fishers of men." How does this call to discipleship differ from the modern "growth track" approach? What are the key elements of true discipleship that might be missing in today's convenience-driven models?

3.   Tim Keller emphasizes discipleship as a lifelong process that involves applying the gospel to every aspect of life. How can churches better support this holistic approach to discipleship, and what changes might be needed in current church practices?

4.   Alan Hirsch argues that the Church exists to make disciples who will make disciples. How can churches shift from a consumer-driven model to a missional model that prioritizes equipping believers for mission? What practical steps can be taken to implement this shift?

5.   Consider how a renewed focus on discipleship can transform leadership within the Church. How does true discipleship lead to more humble, servant-hearted leaders, and how can churches cultivate this type of leadership?

6.   Discuss how discipleship also affects followership. How does discipleship empower believers to be active participants in the mission of the Church, and how can this active followership help prevent the cult of personality in church leadership?

CHAPTER THIRTEEN:

Digital Discipleship – Followership in the Online World

Introduction

The digital age has revolutionized how we communicate, learn, and build relationships. With the rise of social media, online communities, and digital platforms, the Church and broader society have seen a significant shift in the dynamics of leadership and followership. While these technologies offer unprecedented opportunities to spread the gospel and build community, they also present unique challenges. In particular, the digital realm can amplify the voices of celebrity leaders, sometimes at the expense of genuine discipleship and followership.

This chapter explores how the digital age has transformed the landscape of discipleship, examining both the opportunities and risks that come with engaging in online ministry. It also offers strategies for fostering authentic Christian communities in the digital space, where true discipleship can flourish.

The Power of the Tongue in the Digital Age

The Bible speaks extensively about the power of the tongue, emphasizing its potential to build up or tear down. James 3:5-6 warns us of the dangers of unchecked speech: "Likewise, the tongue is a small part of the body, but it makes great boasts. Consider what a great forest is set on fire by a small spark. The tongue also is a fire, a world of evil among the parts of the body. It corrupts the whole body, sets the whole course of one's life on fire, and is itself set on fire by hell."[1]

In the digital age, the power of the tongue has been exponentially amplified. Social media platforms allow individuals to reach vast audiences with a single post, tweet, or video. While this offers incredible potential for sharing the gospel and encouraging others, it also increases the risk of spreading harmful messages, misinformation, or divisive content.[2] The ease with which information can be shared online means that words—both positive and negative—can quickly go viral, shaping public opinion and influencing the behavior of millions.

This reality calls for a heightened sense of responsibility among Christians who engage in digital communication. Just as James warns against the misuse of the tongue, so too must we guard against the misuse of digital platforms. As followers of Christ, we are called to use our words to build up and encourage others, reflecting the love and truth of the gospel in everything we say and share online.[3]

Opportunities and Risks of Digital Discipleship

The digital world presents both opportunities and risks when it comes to discipleship. On the one hand, online platforms offer a powerful means of reaching people with the message of Christ. Churches can livestream services, share sermons and teachings on social media, and connect with believers around the world through online communities. These tools have become especially valuable in times of crisis, such as during the COVID-19 pandemic, when physical gatherings were restricted, and the Church had to rely on digital means to maintain fellowship and ministry.[4]

Opportunities: Expanding the Reach of the Gospel

Digital discipleship allows the Church to reach people who might never step foot in a physical church building. It provides access to biblical teaching, worship, and community for individuals who are geographically isolated, physically unable to attend services, or living in areas where Christianity is restricted. The digital space also enables real-time interaction and engagement, allowing believers to ask questions, share prayer requests, and support one another across distances.[5]

Moreover, online platforms can facilitate lifelong learning and spiritual growth. Believers can access a wealth of resources—Bible studies, podcasts, online courses, and more—tailored to their specific needs and interests. This democratization of knowledge empowers followers to take ownership of their spiritual journey, deepening their understanding of Scripture and their relationship with Christ.[6]

Risks: The Perils of Online Celebrity Culture

However, the digital realm also brings significant risks, particularly the rise of online celebrity culture. In this environment, charismatic leaders can quickly amass large followings, with their teachings and opinions gaining widespread influence. While some of these leaders are faithfully proclaiming the gospel, others may prioritize personal branding, popularity, or controversial takes over sound doctrine and humble service.[7]

This trend can lead to several dangers:

◊ Superficiality in Discipleship: When the focus is on personalities rather than on Christ, discipleship can become shallow and surface-level. Followers may become more attached to a particular leader's style or persona than to the teachings of Jesus, leading to spiritual immaturity and a lack of deep, transformative growth.[8]

◊ Cult of Personality: The elevation of certain leaders to celebrity status can create a "cult of personality," where followers become more loyal to the leader than to the gospel itself. This can lead to divisions within the Church and can even result in followers defending or excusing unbiblical behavior from their chosen leaders.[9]

◊   Misuse of Influence: The vast reach of digital platforms means that a single leader's influence can extend far beyond their immediate community. While this can be positive, it also means that any errors, abuses, or moral failings can have a widespread impact, potentially leading many astray.[10]

Fostering Authentic Christian Communities Online

To counter the risks of online celebrity culture and to harness the opportunities of digital discipleship, it is essential to foster authentic Christian communities in the digital space. This requires intentionality and a commitment to the biblical principles of followership and leadership.

Encouraging True Discipleship

True discipleship is about more than consuming content or following a charismatic leader online. It is about a deep, personal relationship with Jesus Christ and a commitment to growing in His likeness. Churches and Christian leaders can encourage true discipleship online by:

◊   Promoting Accountability: Encourage online communities to practice accountability, where members can hold each other and their leaders to biblical standards. This might involve creating smaller groups within larger online communities where individuals can share their struggles, confess sins, and pray for one another.[11]

◊   Prioritizing Biblical Teaching: Focus on content that is grounded in Scripture and encourages spiritual growth. Avoid sensationalism or clickbait tactics that prioritize views and engagement over truth and substance.[12]

◊   Modeling Humility and Service: Leaders should model the humility and service that Jesus exemplified. Rather than seeking to build their personal brand, they should seek to elevate Christ and point others to Him.[13]

Building Online Communities that Reflect Christ's Teachings

Online communities have the potential to be vibrant, life-giving spaces where believers can grow together in faith. To build such communities, it's important to focus on the following:

◊ Creating Spaces for Meaningful Interaction: Rather than simply broadcasting content, create opportunities for meaningful interaction among community members. This could include discussion forums, live Q&A sessions, virtual prayer meetings, and collaborative projects that allow members to contribute and serve.[14]

◊ Fostering a Culture of Encouragement: As 1 Thessalonians 5:11 urges, "Therefore encourage one another and build each other up, just as in fact you are doing."[15] Online communities should be places of encouragement, where believers can support each other in their walk with Christ. Leaders can model this by affirming the contributions of community members and highlighting stories of faith and growth.[16]

◊ Maintaining a Focus on the Great Commission: In Matthew 28:19-20, Jesus commands His followers to "go and make disciples of all nations." Digital platforms offer an unparalleled opportunity to fulfill this commission. Encourage community members to see their online interactions as a mission field, where they can share the gospel, disciple others, and demonstrate the love of Christ in all they do.[17]

Conclusion: The Future of Digital Discipleship

The digital age presents both challenges and opportunities for the Church. While the rise of online celebrity culture can distort the dynamics of leadership and followership, the digital realm also offers powerful tools for spreading the gospel and building authentic Christian communities. By approaching digital discipleship with intentionality, humility, and a commitment to biblical principles, the Church can harness the potential of digital platforms to cultivate true discipleship and followership.

As we navigate this new landscape, let us be mindful of the words of James 3:5-6 and use our digital platforms to speak life, truth, and encouragement. Let us build communities that reflect the teachings of Christ and empower believers to grow in their faith and make disciples of all nations.

Discussion Questions

1.   How can digital platforms be used to encourage true discipleship and followership, rather than simply amplifying the voices of celebrity leaders? What are some practical strategies for fostering deep spiritual growth in online communities?

2.   What are the potential dangers of online celebrity culture within the Church, and how can followers guard against becoming overly attached to charismatic leaders rather than focusing on Christ?

3.   How can leaders and followers work together to build online communities that reflect Christ's teachings and prioritize accountability, humility, and service? What role does accountability play in maintaining the health of online Christian communities?

CHAPTER FOURTEEN:

Women in Followership – Embracing God's Call in Leadership and Service

Introduction

The role of women in the Church has been a topic of considerable discussion and, at times, controversy. While debates often center on women's leadership, it is equally important to explore the concept of followership and how women have contributed to the life and mission of the Church throughout history. In both leadership and followership, women have played pivotal roles, demonstrating faith, courage, and commitment to God's call.

This chapter will explore the biblical foundation for women in followership, highlight key examples of women in Scripture who embodied this role, and discuss how their example can inform and inspire the Church today. We will also consider how a biblical approach to followership empowers women to lead and serve effectively in various contexts.

Biblical Foundations for Women in Followership

The Bible provides numerous examples of women who played significant roles in God's redemptive plan, often through their faithful followership. From the Old Testament to the New Testament, these women exemplified the virtues of humility, obedience, and boldness in their service to God and others.

Mary, Mother of Jesus: A Model of Obedient Followership

Mary, the mother of Jesus, is one of the most profound examples of obedient followership in Scripture. When the angel Gabriel announced that she would conceive and bear the Son of God, Mary responded with remarkable faith and humility: "I am the Lord's servant," Mary answered. "May your word to me be fulfilled" (Luke 1:38).[1] Despite the potential social and personal risks, Mary embraced God's call, demonstrating a willingness to follow God's plan without hesitation.

Mary's followership was not passive; it required great courage and trust in God. Her role in the incarnation of Christ set the stage for the redemption of humanity, and her example continues to inspire believers to respond to God's call with faith and obedience.[2]

Ruth: Loyalty and Commitment in Followership

Ruth, a Moabite woman, also exemplifies the qualities of followership through her loyalty and commitment. After the death of her husband, Ruth chose to remain with her mother-in-law, Naomi, rather than returning to her own people. Her famous declaration of loyalty is a powerful example of selfless followership: "Where you go I will go, and where you stay I will stay. Your people will be my people and your God my God" (Ruth 1:16).[3]

Ruth's decision to follow Naomi and her God led her to become part of the lineage of King David and, ultimately, Jesus Christ. Her story shows how followership, when aligned with God's will, can lead to extraordinary outcomes and be a part of God's larger plan for redemption.[4]

Priscilla: A Partner in Ministry and Followership

In the New Testament, Priscilla, along with her husband Aquila, is noted for her role in the early Church. Priscilla is mentioned multiple times in the Book of Acts and in Paul's letters, often noted for her hospitality, teaching, and partnership in ministry. One significant moment is when Priscilla and Aquila took Apollos, an eloquent speaker, aside and "explained to him the way of God more accurately" (Acts 18:26).[5]

Priscilla's example illustrates that followership in the early Church was not limited to passive roles but involved active participation in teaching, mentoring, and ministry. Her partnership with Aquila shows the importance of mutual support and collaboration in ministry, embodying the principle of mutual submission that Paul writes about in Ephesians 5:21: "Submit to one another out of reverence for Christ."[6]

The Application of Biblical Followership for Women Today

The examples of Mary, Ruth, and Priscilla demonstrate that followership is not a secondary or inferior role but a vital aspect of God's work in the world. For women today, these examples offer valuable lessons on how to embrace God's call in both leadership and followership.

Embracing a Call to Service

Women in the Church today are called to serve in various capacities, whether in leadership roles, behind-the-scenes ministries, or in everyday acts of service. The key to effective followership is not the visibility of the role but the faithfulness with which it is carried out. Just as Mary, Ruth, and Priscilla embraced their roles with faith and commitment, so too are women today called to serve God and others with wholehearted devotion.[2]

This service may take many forms, from being the set leader, to leadership positions, to mentoring younger women in the faith, to leading small groups, teaching children, or serving in missions. The diversity of these roles reflects the varied gifts and callings that God bestows on His people, and each one is important in the body of Christ.[8]

Supporting and Empowering Others

Biblical followership also involves supporting and empowering others. Just as Ruth supported Naomi and Priscilla partnered with Aquila, women today are called to build up and encourage those around them. This can be done through mentorship, collaboration in ministry, and providing spiritual and emotional support to others in the Church.[9]

Women who embrace a biblical model of followership recognize that their role is not just to follow but to actively contribute to the spiritual growth and well-being of the community. This includes being willing to lead when called upon, as Priscilla did, and to use their gifts to strengthen the Church.[10]

Navigating Challenges in Followership

The path of followership is not without its challenges. Women in the Church may face obstacles such as cultural expectations, limitations in their roles, or struggles with self-doubt. However, the examples of biblical women show that God honors faithful followership, even in the face of adversity.

Women today can draw strength from these examples and from the promises of Scripture, trusting that God equips those He calls. As Philippians 4:13 reminds us, "I can do all this through Him who gives me strength."[11] By relying on God's strength and wisdom, women can navigate the challenges of followership with grace and perseverance.

The Relationship Between Followership and Leadership

One of the key insights from the biblical examples of followership is that it often leads to leadership. Mary's obedience led to her being honored as the mother of Jesus. Ruth's loyalty led her to a place of significance in the lineage of Christ. Priscilla's ministry alongside Aquila made her a respected leader in the early Church.

This demonstrates that followership and leadership are deeply interconnected. Effective leaders are often those who have first learned to follow well. They understand the importance of humility, service, and collaboration, and they lead by example. For women in the Church, embracing followership is not just about fulfilling a role; it is about preparing the heart for whatever leadership God may call them to in the future.[12]

Conclusion: Embracing Followership as a Path to Leadership and Service

The examples of women in Scripture show that followership is a powerful and honorable calling. It is a role that involves faithfulness, courage, and a willingness to serve others. For women in the Church today, embracing this calling means recognizing the value of their contributions, whether in leadership or followership, and seeking to serve God with all their heart.

As the Church continues to grow and evolve, the roles of women in both leadership and followership will remain vital. By following the examples of Mary, Ruth, Priscilla, and others, women can embrace a biblical model of followership that empowers them to lead, serve, and make a lasting impact in the Kingdom of God.

Discussion Questions

1.   Reflect on Mary's response to God's call in Luke 1:38. How does her example challenge or inspire you in your own walk of faith? What does it mean to embrace God's call with humility and obedience?

2.   Ruth's loyalty and commitment to Naomi led her to a significant role in God's redemptive plan. How can Ruth's story inspire women today to commit to relationships and follow God's leading, even when the path is uncertain?

3.   Priscilla was a partner in ministry, actively participating in teaching and mentoring. How does her example challenge traditional views of women's roles in the Church? What can we learn from Priscilla about the relationship between follower-ship and leadership?

4.   How can women in the Church today embrace both leadership and followership as complementary roles? What practical steps can be taken to support and empower women in their callings?

5.   What challenges do women face in followership, and how can they navigate these challenges with faith and perseverance? How can the Church better support women in their roles as followers and leaders?

6.   How does understanding the interconnectedness of followership and leadership change your perspective on both roles? How can this understanding impact the way we serve and lead in our communities?

CHAPTER FIFTEEN:

Ethical Followership – Upholding Integrity in a Complex World

Introduction

In an increasingly complex and morally ambiguous world, the role of ethical followership is more crucial than ever. While much attention is often given to the ethics of leaders, the ethical responsibilities of followers are equally important. Followers, by their actions and decisions, play a vital role in upholding the integrity and mission of the Church. Ethical followership involves more than just obeying leaders; it requires discernment, courage, and a commitment to biblical principles.

This chapter explores the concept of ethical followership, drawing on scriptural foundations and real-world applications. We will examine how followers can contribute to the ethical health of their communities, hold leaders accountable, and influence the Church and society positively.

The Biblical Foundation for Ethical Followership

The Bible provides a robust framework for understanding ethical behavior, not just for leaders but for all believers. Scripture calls us to live lives of integrity, truthfulness, and justice, reflecting the character of Christ in our actions and decisions.

Proverbs 11:3 – The Integrity of the Upright

Proverbs 11:3 states, "The integrity of the upright guides them, but the unfaithful are destroyed by their duplicity."[1] This verse highlights the importance of integrity as a guiding principle in the life of a believer. Integrity involves consistency in moral character, honesty, and adherence to ethical principles, even when it is difficult or unpopular.

For followers, integrity means being faithful to biblical values in all areas of life, including how we relate to leaders and the decisions we make as part of a community. It involves being truthful, reliable, and consistent in our actions regardless of the circumstances.[2]

Micah 6:8 – Acting Justly, Loving Mercy, and Walking Humbly

Micah 6:8 provides a concise summary of what God requires from His people: "He has shown you, O mortal, what is good. And what does the Lord require of you? To act justly and to love mercy and to walk humbly with your God."[3] This verse calls believers to a life of ethical action: acting justly, loving mercy, and walking humbly.

For followers, this means advocating for justice within the Church and society, showing compassion and mercy to others, and maintaining a posture of humility in all interactions. It also implies a responsibility to ensure that our leaders are held to these same standards, encouraging them to lead with justice, mercy, and humility.[4]

Ephesians 4:25 – Speaking the Truth in Love

Ephesians 4:25 instructs believers to "put off falsehood and speak truthfully to your neighbor, for we are all members of one body."[5] Ethical followership involves speaking the truth in love, especially when addressing issues of concern within the Church or community. This includes the courage to confront unethical behavior, to hold leaders accountable, and to do so in a manner that is constructive and loving.

Speaking the truth in love is not about being confrontational for its own sake; it is about seeking the best for others and for the community as a whole. It requires wisdom, discernment, and a deep commitment to the truth of the gospel.[6]

The Role of Ethical Followership in the Church

Ethical followership plays a crucial role in the health and mission of the Church. Followers are not passive recipients of leadership; they are active participants in the life of the Church, responsible for upholding biblical values and contributing to the community's ethical integrity.

Holding Leaders Accountable

One of the most important aspects of ethical followership is holding leaders accountable to biblical standards. While leaders are called to shepherd the flock, followers have a responsibility to ensure that leaders are living and leading according to the principles of Scripture.

Accountability is a two-way street. Just as leaders are accountable to God and to those they lead, followers are accountable for supporting leaders in truth and integrity. This might involve:

◊ Providing Constructive Feedback: Offering feedback to leaders in a way that is respectful and aimed at promoting their growth and effectiveness.[7]

◊ Confronting Unethical Behavior: If a leader is engaging in unethical behavior, followers have a duty to address the issue, seeking to correct it in a manner that is consistent with biblical principles (Matthew 18:15-17).[8]

◊ Supporting Ethical Leadership: Encouraging and supporting leaders who are committed to ethical practices, providing them with the affirmation and resources they need to lead effectively.[2]

Upholding Biblical Values in Decision-Making

Followers also play a critical role in upholding biblical values in decision-making processes within the Church. This includes being involved in discussions and decisions that impact the direction and mission of the Church, ensuring that these decisions align with Scripture.

Ethical followership involves:

◊ Discernment: Applying biblical wisdom and discernment to decisions, ensuring that choices reflect the values of justice, mercy, and humility.[10]

◊ Collaboration: Working collaboratively with leaders and other followers to reach decisions that honor God and serve the community.[11]

◊ Courage: Being willing to stand up for what is right, even when it is unpopular or may come at a personal cost.[12]

Influencing the Broader Community

The impact of ethical followership extends beyond the Church and into the broader community. Followers who live out biblical values in their daily lives become a witness to the world, demonstrating the integrity, justice, and love of Christ.

This influence might be seen in:

◊ Workplace Ethics: Followers who uphold biblical ethics in their workplaces, influencing their colleagues and setting a standard for integrity.[13]

◊ Social Justice Advocacy: Engaging in social justice issues, advocating for the marginalized and oppressed, and working towards systemic change that reflects God's heart for justice.[14]

◊   Community Service: Serving in local communities with humility and compassion, reflecting the love of Christ to those in need.[15]

The Challenges of Ethical Followership

While ethical followership is essential, it is not without its challenges. Followers may face difficulties such as:

◊   Fear of Reprisal: Confronting unethical behavior in leadership can lead to personal risks, including backlash, isolation, or even expulsion from a community.[16]

◊   Moral Ambiguity: In complex situations, it may be difficult to discern the right course of action, requiring deep prayer, consultation with Scripture, and wise counsel.[17]

◊   Cultural Pressures: Followers may face pressure to conform to cultural norms that conflict with biblical values, making it challenging to stand firm in their convictions.[18]

Despite these challenges, ethical followership is crucial for the integrity and witness of the Church. By committing to live and act according to biblical principles, followers contribute to the spiritual health and mission of the Church, ensuring that it remains a faithful reflection of Christ's body on earth.

Application: Practical Steps for Ethical Followership

To practice ethical followership, consider the following steps:

◊   Commit to Personal Integrity: Ensure that your actions and decisions align with biblical principles. Regularly examine your heart and motives, and seek God's guidance in all you do.[19]

◊   Hold Leaders Accountable with Grace: Approach leaders with respect and love, offering feedback and addressing concerns in a manner that is constructive and honors God.[20]

◊　Participate Actively in Church Life: Engage in decision-making processes within your church, ensuring that decisions reflect biblical values and contribute to the mission of the Church.[21]

◊　Advocate for Justice and Mercy: Be a voice for the voiceless, standing up for justice and mercy within your church and community.[22]

◊　Seek Wisdom and Discernment: In complex situations, seek God's wisdom through prayer, Scripture, and counsel from trusted Christian mentors.[23]

Conclusion: The Call to Ethical Followership

Ethical followership is not merely about obeying leaders; it is about actively participating in the mission of the Church with integrity, courage, and a commitment to biblical principles. As followers of Christ, we are called to uphold the values of the Kingdom of God, ensuring that our actions and decisions reflect the character of Christ.

By embracing the call to ethical followership, we contribute to the health and witness of the Church, supporting leaders in their roles and influencing our communities for Christ. In a world that often compromises on ethics, the Church is called to be a beacon of integrity, justice, and love, led by followers who faithfully uphold these values.

Discussion Questions

1.   Proverbs 11:3 speaks of the integrity of the upright. How does this principle apply to your role as a follower in the Church? How can you ensure that your actions consistently reflect integrity?

2.   Micah 6:8 outlines God's requirements for His people: acting justly, loving mercy, and walking humbly. How can these principles guide your decisions and actions as a follower within your church community?

3.   Ephesians 4:25 encourages believers to speak the truth in love. What are some challenges you might face in holding leaders accountable to biblical standards, and how can you approach these situations with both truth and grace?

4.   What practical steps can you take to ensure that ethical followership is a priority in your life? How can you contribute to a culture of integrity and accountability within your church?

5.   How can ethical followership extend beyond the Church and influence your workplace, community, and broader society? What are some specific ways you can reflect biblical ethics in these areas?

6.   Reflect on a time when you faced a moral dilemma as a follower. How did you navigate the situation, and what did you learn about the importance of ethical followership? How can you apply those lessons in the future?

These questions are intended to encourage thoughtful reflection and discussion on the importance of ethical followership, helping readers to consider how they can live out their faith with integrity and contribute to the health and mission of the Church.

CHAPTER SIXTEEN:

Intergenerational Followership – Bridging the Gap Between Generations

Introduction

In the Church, as in any community, there is a natural diversity of age and experience. This diversity presents both challenges and opportunities. Too often, generational differences can lead to misunderstandings, tensions, and even divisions within a church. However, when approached with intentionality and grace, these differences can be a source of strength and vitality, enriching the life of the Church.

Intergenerational followership involves building relationships across generational lines, where older and younger believers learn from and support each other in their walk with Christ. This chapter explores the biblical foundation for intergenerational relationships, highlights the mutual benefits of such relationships, and offers practical steps for fostering a culture of intergenerational followership in the Church.

The Biblical Foundation for Intergenerational Followership

The Bible emphasizes the importance of relationships between generations, particularly in the context of spiritual mentorship and discipleship. Scripture calls both the older and younger generations to actively engage with one another, recognizing the value of shared wisdom and mutual encouragement.

Titus 2:2-8 – Mentorship Across Generations

In his letter to Titus, the Apostle Paul provides specific instructions for how older and younger men and women should interact within the Church:

"Teach the older men to be temperate, worthy of respect, self-controlled, and sound in faith, in love and in endurance. Likewise, teach the older women to be reverent in the way they live, not to be slanderers or addicted to much wine, but to teach what is good. Then they can urge the younger women to love their husbands and children, to be self-controlled and pure, to be busy at home, to be kind, and to be subject to their husbands, so that no one will malign the word of God. Similarly, encourage the young men to be self-controlled. In everything set them an example by doing what is good. In your teaching show integrity, seriousness, and soundness of speech that cannot be condemned, so that those who oppose you may be ashamed because they have nothing bad to say about us" (Titus 2:2-8).[1]

This passage highlights the importance of older believers mentoring and guiding younger believers. Paul emphasizes that older men and women have a responsibility to teach and model godly behavior, while younger believers are encouraged to learn from and follow the example of their elders. This mutual relationship is foundational to the health and growth of the Church.[2]

1 Timothy 4:12 – Valuing the Contributions of Youth

While the wisdom of older generations is invaluable, the Bible also emphasizes the importance of recognizing and valuing the contributions of younger believers. Paul's exhortation to Timothy is a powerful reminder of this:

"Don't let anyone look down on you because you are young, but set an example for the believers in speech, in conduct, in love, in faith and in purity" (1 Timothy 4:12).[3]

This verse reminds us that young believers have an important role to play in the Church. Their energy, fresh perspectives, and passion are vital to the Church's mission. By setting an example in their conduct, young people can inspire and lead others, including those who are older.[4]

Proverbs 20:29 – The Strength of Youth and the Wisdom of Age

The book of Proverbs often highlights the complementary strengths of youth and age. Proverbs 20:29 encapsulates this balance:

"The glory of young men is their strength, gray hair the splendor of the old."[5]

This verse suggests that both youth and age bring valuable contributions to the community. The strength and vitality of youth are essential for the Church's energy and drive, while the wisdom and experience of the older generation provide stability and guidance. Together, these qualities create a balanced and dynamic Church community.[6]

The Benefits of Intergenerational Followership

When the Church embraces intergenerational followership, it fosters a community where every member, regardless of age, is valued and empowered to contribute. This approach brings numerous benefits to both the Church and individual believers.

Wisdom and Experience from Older Generations

Older believers offer a wealth of wisdom and experience that can guide the Church through challenges and uncertainties.

They have walked with the Lord for many years, have faced trials, and have seen God's faithfulness firsthand. Their insights can help younger believers navigate their own spiritual journeys, offering guidance and encouragement.[7]

Mentorship relationships, as outlined in Titus 2, allow older believers to pass on their knowledge and faith to the next generation. This not only strengthens the younger believers but also gives older members a continued sense of purpose and relevance within the Church.[8]

Energy and Innovation from Younger Generations

Younger believers bring energy, innovation, and a fresh perspective to the Church. Their passion for the gospel and eagerness to serve can inspire others and drive the Church forward. They are often more attuned to cultural trends and new technologies, which can be invaluable for outreach and engagement in a rapidly changing world.[9]

By encouraging young believers to take on leadership roles and responsibilities, the Church not only benefits from their strengths but also helps prepare them for future leadership. This investment in younger generations ensures the continuity and growth of the Church.[10]

Mutual Encouragement and Growth

Intergenerational relationships are not just about passing on knowledge from the older to the younger; they are about mutual encouragement and growth. Younger believers can challenge older ones to think in new ways, to be open to change, and to embrace new methods of ministry. Meanwhile, older believers can offer stability, perspective, and a deep understanding of Scripture and theology.[11]

This mutual exchange creates a culture of learning and growth where everyone benefits. The Church becomes a place where all generations are learning from one another, contributing to one another's spiritual growth, and working together for the Kingdom of God.[12]

Practical Steps for Fostering Intergenerational Followership

To foster a culture of intergenerational followership within the Church, intentional steps must be taken to build relationships and create opportunities for cross-generational interaction.

1.   Establish Mentorship Programs: Churches can create formal or informal mentorship programs that pair older and younger believers together. These relationships can be focused on discipleship, spiritual growth, or practical life skills. Mentorship programs provide a structured way for generations to connect and learn from each other.[13]

2.   Encourage Cross-Generational Ministry Teams: By creating ministry teams that intentionally include members of different ages, the Church can foster collaboration and mutual respect. These teams can work on various projects, from outreach initiatives to worship services, bringing together the strengths of each generation.[14]

3.   Promote Intergenerational Worship and Events: Churches can hold intergenerational worship services and events that encourage participation from all age groups. This might include special services where different generations lead worship, share testimonies, or teach. These events can help break down barriers between age groups and build a sense of unity.[15]

4.   Create Spaces for Open Dialogue: Open dialogue between generations is essential for understanding and addressing generational differences. Churches can host forums, discussion groups, or Bible studies where members of all ages can share their perspectives, ask questions, and learn from one

another. These spaces should be safe, respectful, and focused on mutual understanding.[16]

5.   Celebrate the Contributions of All Generations: Churches should make a point of recognizing and celebrating the contributions of all generations. This can be done through special recognition events, testimonials, or simply by regularly affirming the value of each generation's role in the life of the Church. By publicly acknowledging the importance of inter-generational followership, churches can reinforce the message that everyone has something valuable to contribute.[17]

Application: Building Bridges Between Generations

To apply the principles of intergenerational followership, consider taking the following steps:

◊   Seek Out a Mentor or Mentee: Whether you are younger or older, actively seek out a relationship with someone from a different generation. Be intentional about building a connection, learning from each other, and growing together in your faith.[18]

◊   Engage in Cross-Generational Ministry: Volunteer for ministry opportunities that involve working with different age groups. Whether it's teaching a children's class, helping with youth group, or serving alongside older members in a service project, look for ways to build bridges between generations.[19]

◊   Participate in Intergenerational Worship: Attend or help organize worship services or events that include contributions from all generations. Embrace the diversity of experiences and expressions of faith that different age groups bring to worship.[20]

◊   Foster Open Dialogue: Initiate conversations with members of other generations within your church. Ask questions, listen to their stories, and share your own experiences. Be open to learning from their perspectives and offering your insights as well.[21]

◊ Celebrate Generational Diversity: Encourage your church to recognize and celebrate the contributions of different generations. Whether through special events, testimonials, or regular acknowledgments, help create a culture that values and honors all age groups.[22]

Conclusion: The Strength of a United Church

Intergenerational followership is essential for a healthy, vibrant, and united Church. When generations come together to learn from and support one another, the Church becomes stronger, more resilient, and better equipped to fulfill its mission. By bridging the gap between generations, we create a community where every member is valued, every voice is heard, and every gift is used for the glory of God.

As the Church moves forward, let us commit to building relationships across generational lines, fostering a culture of mutual respect, and working together to advance the Kingdom of God. In doing so, we will not only strengthen the Church today but also ensure that it remains strong and faithful for generations to come.

Discussion Questions

1.   Titus 2:2-8 emphasizes the importance of mentorship across generations. How can your church create opportunities for older and younger members to engage in mentoring relationships? What are the benefits of such relationships?

2.   In 1 Timothy 4:12, Paul encourages Timothy to set an example despite his youth. How can younger members of the Church be encouraged to take on leadership roles and responsibilities? What role do older members play in supporting them?

3.   Proverbs 20:29 speaks of the glory of youth and the splendor of age. How can your church ensure that both the strengths of youth and the wisdom of age are valued and utilized? What practical steps can be taken to promote intergenerational collaboration?

4.   What challenges might arise in fostering intergenerational relationships within the Church, and how can they be addressed? How can your church create a culture that values and honors all generations?

5.   How can intergenerational followership contribute to the overall mission and effectiveness of the Church? What role does it play in building a united and resilient community of believers?

6.   Reflect on a time when you learned something valuable from someone of a different generation. How did that experience shape your understanding of followership and community? How can you apply those lessons to your current interactions within the Church?

CHAPTER SEVENTEEN:

Global Followership – Learning from the Worldwide Church

Introduction

The Church of Jesus Christ is a global community, transcending cultural, linguistic, and geographical boundaries. This diversity is not just a testament to the universality of the gospel but also a source of strength and enrichment for the body of Christ. Each culture brings unique perspectives, practices, and understandings of followership that can deepen our collective experience of discipleship. In this chapter, we will explore how learning from the global Church can enhance our understanding of what it means to follow Christ and how we can actively engage in a more interconnected, global expression of faith.

The Biblical Foundation for Global Followership

The Bible provides numerous examples of the gospel crossing cultural and geographical boundaries, demonstrating the importance of a global perspective in the life of the Church. From the Great Commission to the early Church's mission efforts, Scripture emphasizes the unity and diversity of the body of Christ.

Matthew 28:19-20 – The Great Commission

Jesus' command in the Great Commission is foundational to the global mission of the Church:

"Therefore go and make disciples of all nations, baptizing them in the name of the Father and of the Son and of the Holy Spirit, and teaching them to obey everything I have commanded you. And surely I am with you always, to the very end of the age" (Matthew 28:19-20).[1]

This commission emphasizes that the message of Christ is for all nations. The call to "make disciples of all nations" underscores the importance of engaging with diverse cultures and peoples, recognizing that the gospel transcends all human divisions. This command has led to the spread of Christianity across the globe, resulting in a rich diversity of Christian expressions and practices.[2]

Acts 2:5-12 – Pentecost: The Birth of a Global Church

The event of Pentecost recorded in Acts 2 is a powerful example of the global nature of the Church:

"Now there were staying in Jerusalem God-fearing Jews from every nation under heaven. When they heard this sound, a crowd came together in bewilderment, because each one heard their own language being spoken. Utterly amazed, they asked: 'Aren't all these who are speaking Galileans? Then how is it that each of us hears them in our native language? ... We hear them declaring the wonders of God in our own tongues!' Amazed and perplexed, they asked one another, 'What does this mean?'" (Acts 2:5-8, 11-12).[3]

Pentecost marked the birth of the global Church, with people from every nation hearing the gospel in their own language. This event symbolizes the inclusivity and unity of the Church, where diverse cultures and languages are not barriers but are embraced within the body of Christ. The Holy Spirit's work at Pentecost underscores that the message of Christ is meant to be understood and lived out within the context of every culture.[4]

Revelation 7:9 – A Vision of the Global Church

The book of Revelation offers a vision of the global Church in its fullness:

"After this I looked, and there before me was a great multitude that no one could count, from every nation, tribe, people and language, standing before the throne and before the Lamb. They were wearing white robes and were holding palm branches in their hands" (Revelation 7:9).[5]

This vision of the heavenly multitude highlights the diversity and unity of the Church in eternity. It reflects the ultimate fulfillment of the Great Commission, where people from every nation, tribe, and language are gathered together in worship of the Lamb. This vision challenges us to embrace and celebrate the diversity of the global Church today, as a foretaste of the unity we will experience in the Kingdom of God.[6]

Learning from the Global Church

The global Church has much to offer in terms of insights, practices, and perspectives that can enrich our own discipleship and followership. By engaging with the broader body of Christ, we can learn valuable lessons that challenge and expand our understanding of faith.

Embracing Diverse Worship Practices

Worship is expressed in many different ways across the global Church. From the vibrant, expressive worship services in African churches to the contemplative, liturgical practices of Eastern Orthodoxy, these diverse expressions can deepen our own worship experience. Engaging with these different styles can help us appreciate the fullness of worship as an expression of our love for God and can encourage us to incorporate new practices into our own worship life.[7]

Learning from Persecuted Churches

In many parts of the world, Christians face persecution for their faith. The resilience and faithfulness of these believers, often in the face of severe adversity, offer profound lessons in followership. Their commitment to Christ, despite the risks, challenges us to evaluate the depth of our own faith and to stand firm in our convictions. The stories of persecuted Christians remind us of the cost of discipleship and the strength that comes from reliance on the Holy Spirit.[8]

Adopting a Missional Mindset

Many churches in the global South and East have embraced a missional approach to faith, viewing every believer as a missionary in their context. This missional mindset challenges us to see our everyday lives as opportunities for witness and service, regardless of where we live. By learning from these communities, we can cultivate a more outward-focused faith that seeks to engage the world with the love of Christ.[9]

Application: Engaging with the Global Church

To actively engage with the global Church and learn from its diverse expressions of followership, consider the following steps:

1.   Build Relationships with Global Christians: Seek opportunities to connect with believers from different parts of the world. This could be through mission trips, partnerships with international ministries, or simply building relationships with immigrants and refugees in your community. These connections can provide firsthand insights into how faith is lived out in different cultural contexts.[10]

2.   Incorporate Global Perspectives into Worship and Teaching: Encourage your church to incorporate global perspectives into worship and teaching. This might include singing worship songs from different cultures, inviting international speakers, or studying theological writings from global Christian leaders. These practices can broaden your congregation's understanding of the global Church and help create a more inclusive worship experience.[11]

3.   Pray for the Global Church: Make it a regular practice to pray for the global Church, particularly for believers who are facing persecution, poverty, or other challenges. Praying for the global Church helps to cultivate a heart of compassion and solidarity, reminding us that we are part of a much larger body of Christ.[12]

4.   Support Global Missions: Consider how you can support global missions through financial giving, volunteering, or advocacy. By investing in global missions, you are contributing to the spread of the gospel and the strengthening of the global Church. This support can also include raising awareness in your local church about the needs and opportunities in different parts of the world.[13]

5.   Learn from Global Christian Leaders: Read books, listen to sermons, and watch videos from Christian leaders from different parts of the world. Their perspectives can challenge and enrich your own understanding of Scripture and discipleship. Engaging with these voices helps to decentralize Western perspectives and opens you up to the wisdom and insights of the global Church.[14]

Conclusion: Embracing a Global Perspective in Followership

The global Church offers a wealth of wisdom, diversity, and strength that can greatly enrich our own journey of followership. By learning from and engaging with believers from different cultural contexts, we not only broaden our understanding of what it means to follow Christ, but we also contribute to the unity and strength of the body of Christ. As we embrace a global perspective, we reflect the fullness of the gospel, which transcends all human boundaries and brings together people from every nation, tribe, and tongue in worship of the one true God.

Discussion Questions

1.   Matthew 28:19-20, the Great Commission, calls us to make disciples of all nations. How does this command challenge us to engage with the global Church, and what steps can we take to fulfill this mandate in our own lives?

2.   Acts 2:5-12 describes the event of Pentecost, where people from every nation heard the gospel in their own language. How can we embrace the diversity of the global Church in our worship and ministry practices today?

3.   Revelation 7:9 gives us a vision of a diverse multitude worshiping before the throne of God. How can this vision inspire us to pursue greater unity and inclusivity within our local church and in our engagement with the global Church?

4.   What are some practical ways that your church can incorporate global perspectives into its worship, teaching, and ministry? How can these practices deepen your understanding of followership and discipleship?

5.   How can you personally support and engage with the global Church, whether through prayer, relationships, missions, or learning from global Christian leaders? What steps can you take to build connections with believers from different cultural contexts?

6.   Reflect on a time when you learned something valuable from a Christian from a different cultural background. How did that experience shape your understanding of faith and followership? How can you apply those lessons in your own life and community?

CHAPTER EIGHTEEN:

The Power of Followership – Shaping the Future of Leadership

Introduction

Leadership is often celebrated as the driving force behind change, innovation, and progress. However, leadership cannot function effectively in isolation; it is fundamentally dependent on followership. Strong followership is not passive or secondary; it is an active, dynamic force that shapes and even transforms leadership. The future of leadership, particularly within the Church, will be determined by the quality of followership that supports and surrounds it.

In this chapter, we will explore the power of followership and how it influences leadership. We will consider biblical examples that highlight the importance of followership, examine the characteristics of strong followership, and discuss how fostering healthy followership can lead to more effective and sustainable leadership models in the Church and beyond.

The Biblical Foundation for Followership

The Bible provides numerous examples of followership that underscore its importance in God's plan. These examples reveal that followership is not about blind obedience but about active engagement, responsibility, and influence.

Joshua and Moses – Faithful Followership that Leads to Leadership

The relationship between Joshua and Moses offers a powerful example of how faithful followership can shape and prepare one for leadership:

"Now Joshua son of Nun was filled with the spirit of wisdom because Moses had laid his hands on him. So the Israelites listened to him and did what the Lord had commanded Moses." (Deuteronomy 34:9).[1]

Joshua served as Moses's aide for many years, faithfully following and learning from his leadership. His loyalty, obedience, and willingness to support Moses's mission prepared him to eventually lead the Israelites into the Promised Land. Joshua's story illustrates that effective followership can develop the skills, wisdom, and character necessary for future leadership.[2]

Ruth and Naomi – Loyal Followership that Demonstrates Commitment

Ruth's relationship with her mother-in-law Naomi is another example of strong followership that led to significant impact:

"But Ruth replied, 'Don't urge me to leave you or to turn back from you. Where you go I will go, and where you stay I will stay. Your people will be my people and your God my God.'" (Ruth 1:16).[3]

Ruth's decision to stay with Naomi, despite the hardships they faced, demonstrated deep loyalty and commitment. Her followership was not passive but involved active decision-making and sacrifice. Ruth's faithfulness eventually led to her becoming the great-grandmother of King David, placing her in the lineage of Jesus Christ.[4]

The Disciples and Jesus – Transformative Followership

The disciples' relationship with Jesus exemplifies followership that transforms both the followers and the world around them:

"Come, follow me," Jesus said, "and I will send you out to fish for people." At once they left their nets and followed him. (Matthew 4:19-20).[5]

The disciples' willingness to leave everything and follow Jesus was the beginning of a transformative journey. Their followership involved learning from Jesus, growing in their faith, and eventually becoming leaders who would carry the gospel to the ends of the earth. The transformation of these ordinary men into the apostles who established the early Church highlights the profound impact of strong, committed followership.[6]

The Characteristics of Strong Followership

Strong followership is characterized by several key attributes that not only support leadership but also help shape it in positive ways.

1.   Commitment to a Shared Vision

Strong followers are deeply committed to the vision and mission of their community or organization. This commitment is not merely about agreeing with the leader's goals but involves actively working to achieve those goals, often contributing ideas, feedback, and energy to the effort. In the Church, this means being fully invested in the mission to make disciples and advance God's Kingdom.[7]

2.   Integrity and Accountability

Followers with integrity are committed to doing what is right, even when it is difficult. They hold themselves and their leaders accountable to the highest ethical standards. This accountability is crucial in preventing leaders from drifting into unethical behavior or decisions that could harm the community.[8]

3.   Courage to Speak Truth in Love

Strong followers are not afraid to speak up when they see something that needs to be addressed. This might involve offering constructive criticism, challenging decisions that seem unwise, or bringing attention to issues that have been over-looked. Speaking truth in love, as described in Ephesians 4:15, helps ensure that leadership remains aligned with God's will.[9]

4.   Humility and Servanthood

Humility is a key trait of effective followers. They are willing to serve in whatever capacity is needed, without seeking recognition or power. This servant-hearted attitude reflects the example of Christ, who said, "The greatest among you will be your servant" (Matthew 23:11).[10]

5.   Adaptability and Willingness to Grow

Strong followers are adaptable and open to growth. They are willing to learn new skills, take on different roles, and grow in their faith and character. This adaptability is crucial in a rapidly changing world and enables followers to support their leaders more effectively.[11]

The Interplay Between Leadership and Followership

Leadership and followership are deeply interconnected. Strong followership does not just support leadership; it actively shapes it. Here's how:

1.   Influencing Leadership Decisions

Followers often have a closer view of the day-to-day realities and challenges within a community or organization. By providing feedback, insights, and alternative perspectives, followers can help leaders make more informed and effective decisions. This collaborative dynamic strengthens the overall leadership process.[12]

2.   Encouraging Ethical Leadership

Followers who hold their leaders accountable to ethical standards play a crucial role in maintaining the integrity of leadership. This accountability helps prevent moral failures and ensures that leaders are acting in the best interest of the community.[13]

3.   Fostering a Culture of Collaboration

When followers are engaged and proactive, it fosters a culture of collaboration rather than one of hierarchy. Leaders and followers work together as partners in achieving the shared vision. This collaborative culture leads to more innovative solutions and a more united community.[14]

4.   Preparing the Next Generation of Leaders

Strong followership is often the training ground for future leaders. As followers learn from their leaders, they develop the skills, wisdom, and character necessary for leadership. This continuous cycle of followership and leadership ensures the sustainability and growth of the Church and other organizations.[15]

Application: Cultivating Strong Followership

To cultivate strong followership within your church or community, consider the following steps:

1.   Encourage Open Communication

Create an environment where followers feel comfortable sharing their ideas, concerns, and feedback. Open communication builds trust and ensures that leadership is responsive to the needs of the community.[16]

2.   Provide Opportunities for Growth

Offer opportunities for followers to develop their skills and grow in their faith. This might include leadership training, mentoring programs, or roles that allow them to take on more responsibility. Encouraging growth not only benefits the followers but also strengthens the overall leadership.[17]

3.   Model Servant-Hearted Followership

Leaders can model what it means to be a good follower by showing humility, accountability, and a willingness to serve others. When leaders demonstrate these qualities, it sets a powerful example for the entire community.[18]

4.   Recognize and Affirm Contributions

Regularly acknowledge and affirm the contributions of followers. This recognition helps build a sense of value and belonging, motivating followers to continue their active engagement in the mission.[19]

5.   Foster a Collaborative Culture

Promote a culture where leadership and followership are seen as collaborative roles. Encourage teamwork, mutual respect, and a shared commitment to the vision. This collaboration leads to a more cohesive and effective community.[20]

Conclusion: Shaping the Future of Leadership Through Followership

The future of leadership, particularly within the Church, will be shaped by the quality of followership. Strong, ethical, and engaged followership is essential for sustaining healthy leadership and ensuring the effectiveness of the Church's mission. As followers of Christ, we are all called to be active participants in this dynamic process, contributing to the growth and health of the body of Christ.

By embracing the power of followership, we not only support our leaders but also help shape the future of leadership in a way that reflects the values of the Kingdom of God.

The Power of Followership – Shaping the Future of Leadership

As we work together in this collaborative effort, we fulfill our calling to be the hands and feet of Christ in the world, advancing His Kingdom and bringing glory to His name.

Discussion Questions

1.   Reflect on the relationship between Joshua and Moses (Deuteronomy 34:9). How did Joshua's faithful followership prepare him for leadership? What lessons can we learn from Joshua's example about the importance of followership in developing leadership?

2.   Ruth's loyalty to Naomi (Ruth 1:16) demonstrates the power of committed followership. How can we apply Ruth's example of loyalty and commitment in our own roles as followers within the Church?

3.   The disciples' response to Jesus' call (Matthew 4:19-20) led to their transformation into leaders of the early Church. How does this example challenge us to be more committed and active in our followership? How might our followership shape future leadership within the Church?

4.   What are the key characteristics of strong followership? How can we cultivate these traits in ourselves and in our church community?

5.   How can followers influence leadership decisions and encourage ethical leadership? What practical steps can be taken to ensure that leadership and followership are working together effectively?

6.   In what ways can your church foster a culture of collaboration between leaders and followers? What are some specific actions that can be taken to build a stronger, more united community?

END NOTES

INTRODUCTION REFERENCES

[1] Richard S. Dunn, The Age of Religious Wars, 1559-1715 (New York: W.W. Norton & Company, 1979), 20. The concept of the divine right of kings was integral to the political structures of medieval and early modern Europe, where monarchs were seen as God's appointed rulers.

[2] John Locke, Second Treatise of Government, ed. C.B. McPherson (Indianapolis: Hackett Publishing Company, 1980). Locke's ideas on the social contract and the consent of the governed were foundational to modern democratic thought.

[3] Peter F. Drucker, The Practice of Management (New York: Harper & Row, 1954). Drucker is often credited with pioneering modern management practices, which have significantly influenced contemporary leadership models. See also Warren Bennis, On Becoming a Leader (Reading, MA: Addison-Wesley, 1989).

[4] Barbara Kellerman, Followership: How Followers Are Creating Change and Changing Leaders (Boston: Harvard Business Review Press, 2008), 5-7. Kellerman explores how the dynamics of leadership are shifting in a more follower-centric world.

[5] 1 Samuel 9-10; 2 Samuel 7:12-16; 1 Kings 1-2. These chapters detail the divine selection and anointing of Israel's kings,

illustrating the theological framework for kingship in ancient Israel.

[6] Lynn Hunt, The French Revolution and Human Rights: A Brief Documentary History (Boston: Bedford/St. Martin's, 1996), 5-10. The American and French revolutions were pivotal in shifting the understanding of leadership from divine right to popular sovereignty.

[7] Alexis de Tocqueville, Democracy in America, ed. Harvey C. Mansfield and Delba Winthrop (Chicago: University of Chicago Press, 2000). Tocqueville's observations on American democracy highlight the shift from hierarchical to more egalitarian leadership models.

[8] Robert Kelley, The Power of Followership: How to Create Leaders People Want to Follow, and Followers Who Lead Themselves (New York: Doubleday, 1992), 27-30. Kelley argues that effective followers are essential to successful leadership.

[9] Kelley, The Power of Followership, 38-42.

[10] Kellerman, Followership, 3-5. Kellerman's analysis of social media's role in amplifying the voices of followers highlights the shifting dynamics of leadership in the digital age.

[11] Ronald Heifetz, Leadership Without Easy Answers (Cambridge, MA: Harvard University Press, 1994), 15-20. Heifetz discusses how leadership is increasingly defined by the interactions between leaders and followers.

[12] John 13:1-17; Mark 10:45. These passages are foundational to understanding Jesus' model of servant leadership.

[13] Richard J. Foster, Celebration of Discipline: The Path to Spiritual Growth (San Francisco: Harper & Row, 1978), 121-122. Foster emphasizes the importance of humility and service in Christian leadership, drawing from the example of Jesus.

CHAPTER 1 REFERENCES

[1] Richard S. Dunn, The Age of Religious Wars, 1559-1715 (New York: W.W. Norton & Company, 1979), 20. This concept of divine right was deeply rooted in the political and religious structures of medieval Europe and was used to justify the absolute authority of kings.

[2] Gay Robins, The Art of Ancient Egypt (Cambridge, MA: Harvard University Press, 1997), 15-20. Pharaohs were considered gods on earth, embodying both divine and political authority.

[3] Marc Van De Mieroop, A History of the Ancient Near East, ca. 3000-323 BC (Malden, MA: Blackwell Publishing, 2006), 75-78. The Code of Hammurabi is one of the earliest examples of a ruler codifying laws with a claim to divine authority.

[4] 1 Samuel 9-10; 2 Samuel 7:12-16. These passages detail the anointing of Israel's kings by prophets, emphasizing their divine selection.

[5] Marc Van De Mieroop, A History of the Ancient Near East, 77-78.

[6] Richard Bonney, The European Dynastic States, 1494-1660 (Oxford: Oxford University Press, 1991), 293-296. Louis XIV's reign exemplified the idea of absolute monarchy and the divine right of kings.

[7] John Locke, Second Treatise of Government, ed. C.B. Macpherson (Indianapolis: Hackett Publishing Company, 1980), 50-55. Locke's social contract theory was pivotal in moving away from divine right and toward the idea of government by consent.

[8] Jean-Jacques Rousseau, The Social Contract, trans. Maurice Cranston (London: Penguin Classics, 2004), 31-33. Rousseau's

ideas on popular sovereignty further developed the concept of authority derived from the people.

[9] Rousseau, The Social Contract, 52-55.

[10] Charles de Secondat, Baron de Montesquieu, The Spirit of the Laws, trans. Anne M. Cohler, Basia Carolyn Miller, and Harold Samuel Stone (Cambridge: Cambridge University Press, 1989), 157-160. Montesquieu's separation of powers became a fundamental principle in the structure of modern democracies.

[11] Lynn Hunt, The French Revolution and Human Rights: A Brief Documentary History (Boston: Bedford/St. Martin's, 1996), 5-10. The American and French revolutions were deeply influenced by Enlightenment ideals, leading to the establishment of democratic forms of government.

[12] Peter F. Drucker, The Practice of Management (New York: Harper & Row, 1954), 22-25. Drucker's work laid the foundation for modern management and leadership practices.

[13] Drucker, The Practice of Management, 27-30.

[14] Warren Bennis, On Becoming a Leader (Reading, MA: Addison-Wesley, 1989), 35-37. Bennis's distinction between management and leadership has become a fundamental concept in leadership studies.

[15] Max Weber, The Theory of Social and Economic Organization, trans. A.M. Henderson and Talcott Parsons (New York: Oxford University Press, 1947), 358-359. Weber introduced the concept of charismatic authority, which has influenced modern leadership theories.

[16] Barbara Kellerman, Followership: How Followers Are Creating Change and Changing Leaders (Boston: Harvard Business Review Press, 2008), 10-12. Kellerman critiques the overemphasis on individual leadership at the expense of understanding the role of followers.

[17] Daniel Goleman, Emotional Intelligence: Why It Can Matter More Than IQ (New York: Bantam Books, 1995), 95-100. Goleman's work on emotional intelligence has significantly impacted modern leadership theories, particularly the emphasis on relational dynamics and adaptability.

CHAPTER 2 REFERENCES

[1] Richard S. Dunn, The Age of Religious Wars, 1559-1715 (New York: W.W. Norton & Company, 1979), 20. The divine right of kings was a doctrine that asserted the monarch's legitimacy and authority as being directly granted by God.

[2] Ralph Giesey, The Royal Funeral Ceremony in Renaissance France (Geneva: Librairie Droz, 1960), 32-35. The title "Most Christian King" reflected the French monarchs' perceived divine favor and close relationship with the Catholic Church.

[3] Ernst H. Kantorowicz, The King's Two Bodies: A Study in Medieval Political Theology (Princeton: Princeton University Press, 1957), 3-5. This concept was foundational to the medieval understanding of kingship and the sacred nature of the royal bloodline.

[4] Gay Robins, The Art of Ancient Egypt (Cambridge, MA: Harvard University Press, 1997), 15-20. Pharaohs were considered gods on earth, embodying both divine and political authority.

[5] John King Fairbank and Merle Goldman, China: A New History (Cambridge, MA: Harvard University Press, 2006), 42-44. The Mandate of Heaven was a central doctrine in Chinese political philosophy, justifying the emperor's rule and allowing for the legitimate overthrow of a failing dynasty.

[6] Peter Green, Alexander of Macedon, 356–323 B.C.: A Historical Biography (Berkeley: University of California Press, 1991), 202-205. Alexander's military campaigns and the cultural

integration that followed were key to the success and stability of his empire.

[7] Jack Weatherford, Genghis Khan and the Making of the Modern World (New York: Crown Publishers, 2004), 95-98. Genghis Khan's leadership and legal reforms were instrumental in uniting the Mongol tribes and establishing a vast empire.

CHAPTER 3 REFERENCES

[1] John Locke, Second Treatise of Government, ed. C.B. Macpherson (Indianapolis: Hackett Publishing Company, 1980), 50-55. Locke's theory of the social contract was pivotal in moving away from divine right and toward the idea of government by consent.

[2] John Dunn, The Political Thought of John Locke: An Historical Account of the Argument of the 'Two Treatises of Government' (Cambridge: Cambridge University Press, 1982), 102-106. Locke's influence on modern democratic thought is profound and continues to shape our understanding of governance.

[3] Charles de Secondat, Baron de Montesquieu, The Spirit of the Laws, trans. Anne M. Cohler, Basia Carolyn Miller, and Harold Samuel Stone (Cambridge: Cambridge University Press, 1989), 157-160. Montesquieu's ideas on the separation of powers have been foundational in the development of modern constitutional governments.

[4] Bernard Manin, The Principles of Representative Government (Cambridge: Cambridge University Press, 1997), 76-78. The implementation of Montesquieu's ideas in the U.S. Constitution created a system of checks and balances that remains a model for democratic governance.

[5] Jean-Jacques Rousseau, The Social Contract, trans. Maurice Cranston (London: Penguin Classics, 2004), 52-55. Rousseau's

concept of the general will has been a significant influence on democratic theory and practice.

[6] Timothy Tackett, When the King Took Flight (Cambridge, MA: Harvard University Press, 2003), 38-42. Rousseau's ideas were particularly influential during the French Revolution, shaping the revolutionaries' understanding of popular sovereignty.

[7] Gordon S. Wood, The Creation of the American Republic, 1776-1787 (Chapel Hill: University of North Carolina Press, 1969), 132-135. The Founding Fathers drew heavily on Enlightenment ideas in crafting the new American government.

[8] Bernard Bailyn, The Ideological Origins of the American Revolution (Cambridge, MA: Belknap Press of Harvard University Press, 1992), 44-46. The Declaration of Independence reflects Locke's influence, particularly in its emphasis on natural rights.

[9] Simon Schama, Citizens: A Chronicle of the French Revolution (New York: Alfred A. Knopf, 1989), 212-215. The French Revolution was deeply influenced by Enlightenment thought, leading to the radical restructuring of French society and government.

[10] Lynn Hunt, The Family Romance of the French Revolution (Berkeley: University of California Press, 1992), 95-97. The Reign of Terror illustrated the challenges of implementing Rousseau's general will, as the pursuit of collective good sometimes led to the suppression of individual rights.

[11] Immanuel Kant, "An Answer to the Question: What is Enlightenment?" in Practical Philosophy, ed. and trans. Mary J. Gregor (Cambridge: Cambridge University Press, 1996), 17-20. Kant's emphasis on the role of reason and education in the Enlightenment continues to influence modern views on the responsibilities of both leaders and followers.

CHAPTER 4 REFERENCES

[1] John Locke, Second Treatise of Government, ed. C.B. Macpherson (Indianapolis: Hackett Publishing Company, 1980), 50-55. Locke's ideas about natural rights and the social contract were foundational to the American Revolution.

[2] Bernard Bailyn, The Ideological Origins of the American Revolution (Cambridge, MA: Belknap Press of Harvard University Press, 1992), 44-46. The Declaration of Independence reflects Enlightenment principles, particularly those of Locke, regarding equality and government by consent.

[3] Gordon S. Wood, The Creation of the American Republic, 1776-1787 (Chapel Hill: University of North Carolina Press, 1969), 132-135. The U.S. Constitution established a new form of government based on democratic principles and the separation of powers.

[4] Simon Schama, Citizens: A Chronicle of the French Revolution (New York: Alfred A. Knopf, 1989), 212-215. The French Revolution was deeply influenced by Enlightenment thought and marked the decline of absolute monarchy in France.

[5] Lynn Hunt, The French Revolution and Human Rights: A Brief Documentary History (Boston: Bedford/St. Martin's, 1996), 85-88. The Declaration of the Rights of Man and of the Citizen enshrined the principles of popular sovereignty and equality before the law.

[6] Timothy Tackett, When the King Took Flight (Cambridge, MA: Harvard University Press, 2003), 38-42. The Reign of Terror illustrated the challenges of implementing democratic ideals and the dangers of radicalism.

[7] E.P. Thompson, The Making of the English Working Class (New York: Vintage Books, 1966), 194-197. The Reform Acts

in Britain reflected the growing demand for political representation and workers' rights during the Industrial Revolution.

[8] Alexander Keyssar, The Right to Vote: The Contested History of Democracy in the United States (New York: Basic Books, 2000), 142-145. The expansion of suffrage in the United States was a gradual process that reflected the increasing belief in universal representation.

[9] Jean-Jacques Rousseau, The Social Contract, trans. Maurice Cranston (London: Penguin Classics, 2004), 52-55. Rousseau's concept of the general will emphasized that legitimate government must reflect the collective will of the people.

[10] Charles de Secondat, Baron de Montesquieu, The Spirit of the Laws, trans. Anne M. Cohler, Basia Carolyn Miller, and Harold Samuel Stone (Cambridge: Cambridge University Press, 1989), 157-160. Montesquieu's ideas on the separation of powers have been foundational in the development of modern constitutional governments.

[11] A.V. Dicey, Introduction to the Study of the Law of the Constitution (London: Macmillan, 1915), 202-205. The rule of law is a central principle in democratic governance, ensuring that all individuals, including leaders, are subject to the law.

CHAPTER 5 REFERENCES

[1] John Locke, Second Treatise of Government, ed. C.B. Macpherson (Indianapolis: Hackett Publishing Company, 1980), 50-55. Locke's ideas about natural rights and the social contract were foundational to the American Revolution.

[2] Joseph J. Ellis, His Excellency: George Washington (New York: Vintage Books, 2005), 201-205. Washington's leadership during and after the American Revolution set important prece-

dents for the peaceful transition of power and the principles of democratic governance.

[3] Gordon S. Wood, *The Creation of the American Republic, 1776-1787* (Chapel Hill: University of North Carolina Press, 1969), 132-135. The U.S. Constitution established a system of government that institutionalized the democratic ideals of the American Revolution

[4] Simon Schama, Citizens: A Chronicle of the French Revolution (New York: Alfred A. Knopf, 1989), 212-215. The French Revolution sought to dismantle the absolute monarchy and establish a government based on Enlightenment principles.

[5] Lynn Hunt, The French Revolution and Human Rights: A Brief Documentary History (Boston: Bedford/St. Martin's, 1996), 85-88. The Declaration of the Rights of Man and of the Citizenenshrined the principles of popular sovereignty and equality before the law.

[6] David A. Bell, Napoleon: A Concise Biography (New York: Oxford University Press, 2015), 75-80. Napoleon's rise to power illustrates the complexities of revolutionary leadership and the tensions between democratic ideals and authoritarian control.

[7] 7. John Lynch, Simón Bolívar: A Life (New Haven: Yale University Press, 2006), 102-105. Bolívar's leadership in the Latin American revolutions sought to establish independent republics based on the principles of equality and self-determination.

[8] Lester D. Langley, The Americas in the Age of Revolution, 1750-1850 (New Haven: Yale University Press, 1996), 112-115. Bolívar's vision of a united Latin America reflected the challenges of maintaining unity and democracy in the aftermath of revolution.

[9] E. Bradford Burns, The Poverty of Progress: Latin America in the Nineteenth Century (Berkeley: University of California Press, 1980), 45-50. The post-revolutionary struggles in Latin America highlight the difficulties of building stable political institutions after independence.

CHAPTER 6 REFERENCES

[1] Jeffrey Pfeffer, Leadership BS: Fixing Workplaces and Careers One Truth at a Time (New York: Harper Business, 2015), 11-14. Pfeffer discusses the commodification of leadership and the rise of the leadership industry.

[2] James MacGregor Burns, Leadership (New York: Harper & Row, 1978), 2-3. Burns explores how leadership evolved into a distinct and professional enterprise.

[3] James 4:13-14 (NIV).

[4] Peter F. Drucker, The Practice of Management (New York: Harper & Row, 1954), 23-25. Drucker's work laid the foundation for modern management and leadership practices, emphasizing efficiency and organizational goals.

[5] Barbara Kellerman, The End of Leadership (New York: Harper Business, 2012), 18-20. Kellerman critiques the reductionist view of leadership that focuses primarily on outcomes and metrics.

[6] Mark 10:42-45 (NIV).

[7] John C. Maxwell, The 21 Irrefutable Laws of Leadership (Nashville: Thomas Nelson, 2007), 7-8. Maxwell emphasizes the importance of servant leadership as a counter to the traditional, top-down approach.

[8] Jeffrey Pfeffer, Leadership BS: Fixing Workplaces and Careers One Truth at a Time (New York: Harper Business, 2015), 5-6. Pfeffer highlights the commercialization of leadership and its impact on the practice of leading.

[9] 1 Timothy 6:10 (NIV).

[10] Henri J.M. Nouwen, In the Name of Jesus: Reflections on Christian Leadership (New York: Crossroad, 1989), 17-19. Nouwen reflects on the dangers of leadership driven by ego and personal success rather than service.

[11] Matthew 25:14-30 (NIV).

[12] R. Paul Stevens, The Other Six Days: Vocation, Work, and Ministry in Biblical Perspective (Grand Rapids: Eerdmans, 1999), 105-108. Stevens discusses the concept of stewardship in the context of Christian vocation and work.

[13] Dallas Willard, The Divine Conspiracy: Rediscovering Our Hidden Life in God (San Francisco: HarperSanFrancisco, 1998), 291-293. Willard emphasizes accountability in leadership and the importance of aligning leadership practices with God's purposes.

[14] Philippians 2:3-4 (NIV).

[15] Robert K. Greenleaf, Servant Leadership: A Journey into the Nature of Legitimate Power and Greatness (Mahwah, NJ: Paulist Press, 1977), 13-15. Greenleaf's seminal work on servant leadership offers a model for leading in a way that prioritizes service and humility over power and control.

CHAPTER 7 REFERENCES

[1] Walter Brueggemann, First and Second Samuel (Louisville: Westminster John Knox Press, 1990), 119-121.

[2] Robert D. Putnam, Bowling Alone: The Collapse and Revival of American Community (New York: Simon & Schuster, 2000), 23-26.

[3] Bethany McLean and Peter Elkind, The Smartest Guys in the Room: The Amazing Rise and Scandalous Fall of Enron (New

York: Portfolio, 2003), 85-88; Joseph E. Stiglitz, Freefall: America, Free Markets, and the Sinking of the World Economy (New York: W.W. Norton & Company, 2010), 29-31.

[4] Richard B. Hays, The Moral Vision of the New Testament: A Contemporary Introduction to New Testament Ethics (New York: HarperOne, 1996), 342-344.

[5] Ibid.

[6] Mark Chaves, American Religion: Contemporary Trends (Princeton: Princeton University Press, 2011), 40-43.

[7] Walter Brueggemann, Theology of the Old Testament: Testimony, Dispute, Advocacy (Minneapolis: Fortress Press, 1997), 645-647.

[8] Ibid.

[9] Bruce K. Waltke, The Book of Proverbs: Chapters 15-31 (Grand Rapids: Eerdmans, 2005), 395-397.

[10] Douglas J. Moo, The Letter of James (Grand Rapids: Eerdmans, 2000), 135-137.

[11] John C. Maxwell, The 21 Irrefutable Laws of Leadership: Follow Them and People Will Follow You (Nashville: Thomas Nelson, 2007), 75-77.

[12] Dietrich Bonhoeffer, Life Together (New York: Harper & Row, 1954), 89-91.

[13] Robert K. Greenleaf, Servant Leadership: A Journey into the Nature of Legitimate Power and Greatness (Mahwah, NJ: Paulist Press, 1977), 11-13.

CHAPTER 8 REFERENCES

[1] Paul, 1 Corinthians 12:12-14, New International Version.

[2] The story of the Israelites following Moses is extensively explored in biblical commentaries, including Walter Brueggemann, The Book of Exodus (New York: Cambridge University Press, 1994), 185-187.

[3] The consequences of the Israelites' poor followership are detailed in Numbers 14:1-4, 20-23.

[4] Matthew 4:19, New International Version.

[5] Matthew 28:19-20, New International Version.

[6] Ephesians 5:21, New International Version.

[7] John 13:12-15, New International Version.

[8] The potential for conflict and power struggles in followership is discussed in Edwin P. Hollander, Inclusive Leadership: The Essential Leader-Follower Relationship (New York: Routledge, 2009), 99-101.

[9] The importance of mutual submission and collective influence is emphasized in Dietrich Bonhoeffer, Life Together (New York: Harper & Row, 1954), 57-59.

CHAPTER 9 REFERENCES

[1] Matthew 20:25-28, New International Version.

[2] John 13:12-15, New International Version.

[3] The concept of servant leadership as modeled by Jesus is discussed in Robert K. Greenleaf, Servant Leadership: A Journey into the Nature of Legitimate Power and Greatness (Mahwah, NJ: Paulist Press, 1977), 21-23.

[4] Philippians 2:5-8, New International Version.

[5] The humility of Christ in the incarnation and the cross is a central theme in Dietrich Bonhoeffer, The Cost of Discipleship (New York: Touchstone, 1995), 87-89.

[6] Humility in leadership and its application in modern contexts is explored in Jim Collins, Good to Great: Why Some Companies Make the Leap... and Others Don't (New York: HarperBusiness, 2001), 37-40.

[7] John 10:11, New International Version.

[8] Romans 5:8, New International Version.

[9] The implications of sacrificial love for leadership are discussed in Henri J.M. Nouwen, In the Name of Jesus: Reflections on Christian Leadership (New York: Crossroad, 1989), 27-29.

[10] John 13:34-35, New International Version.

CHAPTER 10 REFERENCES

[1] Mark 10:42-45, New International Version.

[2] The principles and application of servant leadership are discussed in Robert K. Greenleaf, Servant Leadership: A Journey into the Nature of Legitimate Power and Greatness (Mahwah, NJ: Paulist Press, 1977), 25-27.

[3] Matthew 8:5-13, New International Version.

[4] The role of humility in leadership and its implications for modern practices are explored in Jim Collins, Good to Great: Why Some Companies Make the Leap... and Others Don't (New York: HarperBusiness, 2001), 33-36.

[5] Matthew 4:10-11, New International Version.

[6] The challenges of maintaining ethical integrity in leadership are discussed in Max De Pree, Leadership Is an Art (New York: Doubleday, 1989), 85-87.

[7] Acts 2:42-47, New International Version.

[8] The potential of servant leadership to transform organizations and communities is highlighted in James C. Hunter, The Servant: A Simple Story About the True Essence of Leadership (New York: Crown Business, 1998), 49-51.

CHAPTER 11 REFERENCES

[1] Matthew 20:28, New International Version.

[2] The concept of leadership as servanthood is further explored in Robert K. Greenleaf, Servant Leadership: A Journey into the Nature of Legitimate Power and Greatness (Mahwah, NJ: Paulist Press, 1977), 20-23.

[3] Philippians 2:5-8, New International Version.

[4] The importance of humility in leadership is discussed in Jim Collins, Good to Great: Why Some Companies Make the Leap... and Others Don't (New York: HarperBusiness, 2001), 37-39.

[5] Ephesians 5:21, New International Version.

[6] Collective influence and its application in leadership are explored in Edwin P. Hollander, Inclusive Leadership: The Essen-

tial Leader-Follower Relationship (New York: Routledge, 2009), 102-105.

[7] John 13:14-15, New International Version.

[8] The transformative potential of Jesus' leadership model in modern contexts is discussed in Henri J.M. Nouwen, In the Name of Jesus: Reflections on Christian Leadership (New York: Crossroad, 1989), 31-33.

[9] The impact of servant leadership on inclusive and ethical decision-making is highlighted in James C. Hunter, The Servant: A Simple Story About the True Essence of Leadership (New York: Crown Business, 1998), 53-55.

[10] The challenges and opportunities of modern servant leadership are discussed in Max De Pree, Leadership Is an Art (New York: Doubleday, 1989), 92-94.

[11] Nehemiah 2:17-18, New International Version.

[12] Nehemiah's leadership model and its implications for today are explored in Walter Brueggemann, Hopeful Imagination: Prophetic Voices in Exile (Philadelphia: Fortress Press, 1986), 65-67.

[13] Practical applications of servant leadership principles are discussed in John C. Maxwell, The 21 Irrefutable Laws of Leadership: Follow Them and People Will Follow You (Nashville: Thomas Nelson, 2007), 82-85.

CHAPTER 12 REFERENCES

[1] Matthew 4:19, New International Version.

[2] The influence of celebrity culture on the church is discussed in Skye Jethani, The Divine Commodity: Discovering a Faith

Beyond Consumer Christianity (Grand Rapids, MI: Zondervan, 2009), 42-45.

[3] The focus on branding and large-scale church marketing is examined in Chris Hodges, The Daniel Dilemma: How to Stand Firm and Love Well in a Culture of Compromise (Nashville, TN: Thomas Nelson, 2017), 83-86.

[4] 1 Corinthians 1:12-13, New International Version.

[5] The trend of reducing discipleship to programs is critiqued in Michael Horton, Christless Christianity: The Alternative Gospel of the American Church (Grand Rapids, MI: Baker Books, 2008), 123-125.

[6] The depth of true discipleship is explored in Dietrich Bonhoeffer, The Cost of Discipleship (New York: Simon & Schuster, 1959), 87-90.

[7] Tim Keller, Center Church: Doing Balanced, Gospel-Centered Ministry in Your City (Grand Rapids, MI: Zondervan, 2012), 108-110.

[8] Alan Hirsch, The Forgotten Ways: Reactivating the Missional Church (Grand Rapids, MI: Brazos Press, 2006), 132-134.

[9] Hirsch, The Forgotten Ways, 135.

[10] The shift towards a missional approach is discussed in Reggie McNeal, Missional Renaissance: Changing the Scorecard for the Church (San Francisco: Jossey-Bass, 2009), 98-100.

[11] The impact of convenience culture on discipleship is analyzed in Kyle Idleman, Not a Fan: Becoming a Completely Committed Follower of Jesus (Grand Rapids, MI: Zondervan, 2011), 73-75.

[12] Romans 12:2, New International Version.

[13] Luke 14:27, New International Version.

[14] The connection between discipleship and biblical leadership is explored in Robert E. Coleman, The Master Plan of Evangelism (Grand Rapids, MI: Revell, 2006), 49-51.

[15] John 13:14-15, New International Version.

[16] Biblical leadership principles are discussed in John C. Maxwell, The 21 Irrefutable Laws of Leadership: Follow Them and People Will Follow You (Nashville, TN: Thomas Nelson, 2007), 92-95.

[17] Ephesians 4:15-16, New International Version.

[18] The role of active followership in the church is highlighted in Barbara Kellerman, The End of Leadership (New York: Harper-Business, 2012), 102-105.

[19] Acts 2:42 47, New International Version.

[20] The importance of authentic community in discipleship is discussed in Dietrich Bonhoeffer, Life Together (New York: Harper & Row, 1954), 29-32.

[21] Spiritual formation as a lifelong journey is explored in Dallas Willard, *The Spirit of the Disciplines: Understanding How Christ Changes Lives* (San Francisco: HarperOne, 1988), 85-88.

[22] Practical approaches to spiritual formation within the church are discussed in Richard J. Foster, Celebration of Discipline: The Path to Spiritual Growth (San Francisco: Harper & Row, 1978), 149-151.

[23] The missional church model and its focus on discipleship are elaborated in Alan Hirsch, The Forgotten Ways: Reactivating the Missional Church (Grand Rapids, MI: Brazos Press, 2006), 145-148.

[24] Practical steps for equipping believers for mission are discussed in Rick Warren, The Purpose Driven Church: Growth Without Compromising Your Message & Mission (Grand Rapids, MI: Zondervan, 1995), 202-205.

[25] Matthew 4:19, New International Version.

CHAPTER 13 REFERENCES

[1] James 3:5-6, New International Version.

[2] The impact of digital communication on public discourse is explored in Clay Shirky, Here Comes Everybody: The Power of Organizing Without Organizations (New York: Penguin Press, 2008), 85-88.

[3] The responsibility of Christians in online communication is discussed in Tony Reinke, 12 Ways Your Phone Is Changing You (Wheaton, IL: Crossway, 2017), 56-59.

[4] The role of digital platforms during the COVID-19 pandemic is analyzed in Heidi A. Campbell, ed., *The Distanced Church: Reflections onDoing Church Online* (Digital Religion Publications, 2020), 22-25.

[5] The potential of digital discipleship is highlighted in Nona Jones, From Social Media to Social Ministry: A Guide to Digital Discipleship (Grand Rapids, MI: Zondervan, 2020), 77-80.

[6] The democratization of religious knowledge through online platforms is discussed in Elizabeth Drescher, Tweet If You ⍰ Jesus: Practicing Church in the Digital Reformation (New York: Morehouse Publishing, 2011), 99-102.

[7] The rise of online celebrity culture is critiqued in Kate Bowler, Blessed: A History of the American Prosperity Gospel (New York: Oxford University Press, 2013), 112-115.

[8] Superficiality in online discipleship is explored in Chris Stedman, IRL: Finding Realness, Meaning, and Belonging in Our Digital Lives (New York: Broadleaf Books, 2020), 48-51.

[9] The dangers of the "cult of personality" in religious leadership are discussed in Carl R. Trueman, The Rise and Triumph of the Modern Self (Wheaton, IL: Crossway, 2020), 133-136.

[10] The misuse of influence in online ministries is analyzed in Steven Furtick, Unqualified: How God Uses Broken People to Do Big Things (Colorado Springs, CO: Multnomah, 2016), 65-68.

[11] Accountability in online communities is emphasized in Michael Hyatt and Megan Hyatt Miller, Win at Work and Succeed at Life: 5 Principles to Free Yourself from the Cult of Overwork (Grand Rapids, MI: Baker Books, 2021), 132-135.

[12] The importance of prioritizing biblical teaching over sensationalism is highlighted in David Platt, Counter Culture: Following Christ in an Anti-Christian Age (Carol Stream, IL: Tyndale House Publishers, 2015), 89-92.

[13] The modeling of humility and service in online leadership is discussed in John C. Maxwell, The 5 Levels of Leadership: Proven Steps to Maximize Your Potential (New York: Center Street, 2011), 144-147.

[14] Strategies for creating meaningful interaction in digital spaces are explored in Bethany Jett and Michelle Medlock Adams, They Call Me Mom: 52 Encouraging Devotions for Every Moment (Grand Rapids, MI: Kregel Publications, 2019), 97-100.

[15] 1 Thessalonians 5:11, New International Version.

[16] The culture of encouragement in online communities is discussed in John Burke, No Perfect People Allowed: Creating a Come-as-You-Are Culture in the Church (Grand Rapids, MI: Zondervan, 2005), 154-157.

[17] Matthew 28:19-20, New International Version.

CHAPTER 14 REFERENCES

[1] Luke 1:38, New International Version.

[2] The significance of Mary's response to God's call is discussed in Scot McKnight, The Real Mary: Why Evangelical Christians Can Embrace the Mother of Jesus (Brewster, MA: Paraclete Press, 2007), 45-48.

[3] Ruth 1:16, New International Version.

[4] The role of Ruth in the lineage of Christ is highlighted in Carolyn Custis James, The Gospel of Ruth: Loving God Enough to Break the Rules (Grand Rapids, MI: Zondervan, 2008), 82-85.

[5] Acts 18:26, New International Version.

[6] The significance of Priscilla's ministry is discussed in Ben Witherington III, Priscilla: The Life of an Early Christian (Grand Rapids, MI: Eerdmans, 2003), 121-124.

[7] The diversity of women's roles in the Church is explored in Alice Mathews, Gender Roles and the People of God: Rethinking What We Were Taught about Men and Women in the Church (Grand Rapids, MI: Zondervan, 2017), 156-159.

[8] The importance of varied gifts in the body of Christ is emphasized in Marg Mowczko, The Ministry of Women in the New Testament: Reclaiming the Biblical Vision for Church Leadership (Grand Rapids, MI: Zondervan, 2020), 97-100.

[9] The role of mentorship and collaboration in ministry is discussed in Sharon Hodde Miller, Nice: Why We Love to Be Liked and How God Calls Us to More (Nashville, TN: B&H Publishing, 2019), 62-65.

[10] The concept of active contribution in biblical followership is explored in Lynn Cohick, Women in the World of the Earliest

Christians: Illuminating Ancient Ways of Life (Grand Rapids, MI: Baker Academic, 2009), 184-187.

[11] Philippians 4:13, New International Version.

[12] The interconnectedness of followership and leadership is discussed in Jo Saxton, The Dream of You: Let Go of Broken Identities and Live the Life You Were Made For (Colorado Springs, CO: WaterBrook, 2018), 144-147.

CHAPTER 15 REFERENCES

[1] Proverbs 11:3, New International Version.

[2] The importance of integrity in the life of a believer is discussed in Jerry Bridges, The Practice of Godliness (Colorado Springs, CO: NavPress, 1983), 157-159.

[3] Micah 6:8, New International Version.

[4] The role of justice, mercy, and humility in ethical behavior is explored in Timothy Keller, Generous Justice: How God's Grace Makes Us Just (New York: Riverhead Books, 2010), 94-97.

[5] Ephesians 4:25, New International Version.

[6] The concept of speaking the truth in love is discussed in Henry Cloud, Integrity: The Courage to Meet the Demands of Reality (New York: HarperCollins, 2006), 121-123.

[7] The importance of providing constructive feedback in leadership is highlighted in John C. Maxwell, The 360 Degree Leader: Developing Your Influence from Anywhere in the Organization (Nashville, TN: Thomas Nelson, 2005), 189-192.

[8] Confronting unethical behavior within the Church is discussed in Dan Allender, Leading with a Limp: Turning Your

Struggles into Strengths (Colorado Springs, CO: WaterBrook Press, 2006), 145-148.

[9] Supporting ethical leadership is emphasized in Richard Blackaby and Henry Blackaby, Spiritual Leadership: Moving People on to God's Agenda (Nashville, TN: B&H Publishing Group, 2011), 215-218.

[10] Discernment in decision-making processes is explored in J. I. Packer, Knowing God (Downers Grove, IL: InterVarsity Press, 1973), 102-104.

[11] Collaboration in church leadership is discussed in L. Gregory Jones, Christian Social Innovation: Renewing Wesleyan Witness (Nashville, TN: Abingdon Press, 2016), 82-85.

[12] The courage to stand for biblical values is discussed in Eric Metaxas, Bonhoeffer: Pastor, Martyr, Prophet, Spy (Nashville, TN: Thomas Nelson, 2010), 307-310.

[13] The impact of ethical behavior in the workplace is highlighted in Dallas Willard, The Divine Conspiracy: Rediscovering Our Hidden Life in God (San Francisco, CA: HarperCollins, 1998), 230-233.

[14] The role of followers in social justice is explored in N. T. Wright, Simply Christian: Why Christianity Makes Sense (New York: HarperOne, 2006), 190-193.

[15] Community service as a reflection of Christ's love is discussed in Richard J. Foster, Celebration of Discipline: The Path to Spiritual Growth (New York: HarperCollins, 1988), 175-178.

[16] The challenges of confronting unethical leadership are explored in Ronald A. Heifetz and Marty Linsky, Leadership on the Line: Staying Alive Through the Dangers of Leading (Boston, MA: Harvard Business Review Press, 2002), 132-135.

[17] Navigating moral ambiguity in leadership is discussed in Alasdair MacIntyre, After Virtue: A Study in Moral Theory

(Notre Dame, IN: University of Notre Dame Press, 1981), 250-253.

[18] The pressures to conform to cultural norms and how to resist them is explored in Os Guinness, Impossible People: Christian Courage and the Struggle for the Soul of Civilization (Downers Grove, IL: InterVarsity Press, 2016), 198-201.

[19] Personal integrity in leadership is highlighted in Bill Hybels, Who You Are When No One's Looking: Choosing Consistency, Resisting Compromise (Downers Grove, IL: InterVarsity Press, 1995), 67-70.

[20] The approach to holding leaders accountable is discussed in Andy Stanley, Next Generation Leader: Five Essentials for Those Who Will Shape the Future (Colorado Springs, CO: Multnomah Books, 2003), 158-160.

[21] Participating actively in church decision-making is emphasized in Eugene H. Peterson, The Contemplative Pastor: Returning to the Art of Spiritual Direction (Grand Rapids, MI: Eerdmans, 1989), 111-113.

[22] Advocating for justice and mercy within the church is explored in Cornel West, Democracy Matters: Winning the Fight Against Imperialism (New York: Penguin Press, 2004), 142-145.

[23] The need for wisdom and discernment in complex situations is discussed in Charles H. Spurgeon, Lectures to My Students (Grand Rapids, MI: Zondervan, 1954), 219-221.

CHAPTER 16 REFERENCES

[1] Titus 2:2-8, New International Version.

[2] The importance of intergenerational mentorship in the Church is discussed in Howard Hendricks, Teaching to Change Lives (Colorado Springs, CO: Multnomah Books, 1987), 78-80.

[3] 1 Timothy 4:12, New International Version.

[4] The role of young leaders in the Church is explored in Tim Elmore, Generation iY: Secrets to Connecting with Today's Teens & Young Adults in the Digital Age (Atlanta, GA: Poet Gardener Publishing, 2010), 145-147.

[5] Proverbs 20:29, New International Version.

[6] The balance between youth and age in the Church is discussed in Leonard Sweet, The Well-Played Life: Why Pleasing God Doesn't Have to Be Such Hard Work (Carol Stream, IL: Tyndale Momentum, 2014), 159-162.

[7] The significance of wisdom from older generations is highlighted in J.I. Packer, Finishing Our Course with Joy: Guidance from God for Engaging with Our Aging (Wheaton, IL: Crossway, 2014), 112-115.

[8] The importance of passing on faith to the next generation is discussed in Susan Hunt, Spiritual Mothering: The Titus 2 Model for Women Mentoring Women (Wheaton, IL: Crossway, 2009), 92-95.

[9] The impact of younger generations on Church innovation is explored in David Kinnaman and Gabe Lyons, Unchristian:

What a New Generation Really Thinks About Christianity... and Why It Matters (Grand Rapids, MI: Baker Books, 2007), 184-186.

[10] Preparing young believers for future leadership is discussed in Jeffrey Arnold, Seven Traits of a Successful Leader (Downers Grove, IL: InterVarsity Press, 2005), 98-101.

[11] The mutual growth in intergenerational relationships is high-lighted in Richard L. Dunn and Jana L. Sundene, Shaping the Journey of Emerging Adults: Life-Giving Rhythms for Spiritual Transformation (Downers Grove, IL: InterVarsity Press, 2012), 138-141.

[12] Building a culture of mutual learning and growth is discussed in Christine Yount Jones, Intergenerational Ministry: Why and How We Pass on Our Faith to the Next Generation (Loveland, CO: Group Publishing, 2014), 45-48.

[13] The benefits of mentorship programs are explored in Lois J. Zachary, The Mentor's Guide: Facilitating Effective Learning Relationships (San Francisco, CA: Jossey-Bass, 2000), 165-168.

[14] The value of cross-generational ministry teams is discussed in Kara Powell, Growing Young: Six Essential Strategies to Help Young People Discover and Love Your Church (Grand Rapids, MI: Baker Books, 2016), 109-112.

[15] Promoting intergenerational worship and events is explored in Holly Catterton Allen and Christine Lawton Ross, Intergen-erational Christian Formation: Bringing the Whole Church To-gether in Ministry, Community, and Worship (Downers Grove, IL: InterVarsity Press, 2012), 93-96.

[16] Creating spaces for open dialogue between generations is discussed in Mary Kate Morse, Making Room for Leadership: Power, Space, and Influence (Downers Grove, IL: InterVarsity Press, 2008), 123-126.

[17] The importance of celebrating generational diversity is explored in James Emery White, Meet Generation Z: Understanding and Reaching the New Post-Christian World (Grand Rapids, MI: Baker Books, 2017), 143-146.

[18] The steps for building intergenerational connections are highlighted in Sharon Galgay Ketcham, Reciprocal Church: Becoming a Community Where Faith Flourishes Beyond High School (Downers Grove, IL: InterVarsity Press, 2018), 87-90.

[19] Engaging in cross-generational ministry is discussed in Allen and Ross, Intergenerational Christian Formation, 102-105.

[20] The value of intergenerational worship is explored in the same work by Allen and Ross, Intergenerational Christian Formation, 138-141.

[21] Initiating conversations with different generations is discussed in the same work by Ketcham, Reciprocal Church, 115-117.

[22] Celebrating generational diversity and its importance is discussed in White, Meet Generation Z, 157-160.

CHAPTER 17 REFERENCES

[1] Matthew 28:19-20, New International Version.

[2] The importance of global mission in fulfilling the Great Commission is discussed in John Piper, Let the Nations Be Glad! (Grand Rapids, MI: Baker Academic, 2010), 35-37.

[3] Acts 2:5-12, New InternationalVersion.

[4] The significance of Pentecost in the global Church is explored in Craig S. Keener, Acts: An Exegetical Commentary (Grand Rapids, MI: Baker Academic, 2012), 979-981.

[5] Revelation 7:9, New International Version.

[6] The vision of the global Church in Revelation is discussed in Richard Bauckham, The Theology of the Book of Revelation (Cambridge: Cambridge University Press, 1993), 93-95.

[7] The diversity of worship practices in the global Church is highlighted in Robert E. Webber, Ancient-Future Worship: Proclaiming and Enacting God's Narrative (Grand Rapids, MI: Baker Books, 2008), 134-136.

[8] Lessons from persecuted churches are discussed in Nik Ripken, The Insanity of God: A True Story of Faith Resurrected (Nashville, TN: B&H Books, 2013), 221-224.

[9] The missional mindset of the global Church is explored in Christopher J. H. Wright, The Mission of God: Unlocking the Bible's Grand Narrative (Downers Grove, IL: IVP Academic, 2006), 67-69.

[10] Building relationships with global Christians is discussed in David Livermore, Cultural Intelligence: Improving Your CQ to Engage Our Multicultural World (Grand Rapids, MI: Baker Academic, 2009), 179-181.

[11] Incorporating global perspectives into worship and teaching is explored in Richard Mouw and Douglas Sweeney, The Suffering and Victorious Christ: Toward a More Compassionate Christology (Grand Rapids, MI: Baker Academic, 2013), 94-97.

[12] The importance of praying for the global Church is highlighted in Patrick Johnstone, Operation World: The Definitive Prayer Guide to Every Nation (Downers Grove, IL: IVP Books, 2010), 23-25.

[13] Supporting global missions is discussed in Andy Johnson, Missions: How the Local Church Goes Global (Wheaton, IL: Crossway, 2017), 101-104.

[14] Learning from global Christian leaders is explored in Lamin Sanneh, Whose Religion Is Christianity? The Gospel beyond the West (Grand Rapids, MI: Eerdmans, 2003), 81-83.

CHAPTER 18 REFERENCES

[1] Deuteronomy 34:9, New International Version.

[2] The relationship between Joshua and Moses is explored in Richard S. Hess, Joshua: An Introduction and Commentary (Downers Grove, IL: InterVarsity Press, 1996), 49-51.

[3] Ruth 1:16, New International Version.

[4] Ruth's loyalty and its significance are discussed in Daniel I. Block, Ruth: The King Is Coming (Nashville, TN: B&H Publishing Group, 2019), 41-43.

[5] Matthew 4:19-20, New International Version.

[6] The transformative followership of the disciples is explored in R. T. France, The Gospel of Matthew (Grand Rapids, MI: Eerdmans, 2007), 159-161.

[7] The commitment to a shared vision is emphasized in Leonard Sweet, I Am a Follower: The Way, Truth, and Life of Following Jesus (Nashville, TN: Thomas Nelson, 2012), 85-87.

[8] Integrity and accountability in followership are discussed in Barbara Kellerman, Followership: How Followers Are Creating Change and Changing Leaders (Boston, MA: Harvard Business Review Press, 2008), 112-114.

[9] Speaking truth in love as a characteristic of strong followership is highlighted in Joseph H. Hellerman, When the Church Was a Family: Recapturing Jesus' Vision for Authentic Christian Community (Nashville, TN: B&H Academic, 2009), 144-146.

[10] Humility and servanthood in followership are modeled in John Dickson, Humilitas: A Lost Key to Life, Love, and Leadership (Grand Rapids, MI: Zondervan, 2011), 101-103.

[11] Adaptability and willingness to grow are important aspects of followership, as discussed in Ira Chaleff, The Courageous Follower: Standing Up to and for Our Leaders (San Francisco, CA: Berrett-Koehler Publishers, 2009), 87-89.

[12] The role of followership in influencing leadership decisions is explored in Ronald E. Riggio, Ira Chaleff, and Jean Lipman-Blumen, The Art of Followership: How Great Followers Create Great Leaders and Organizations (San Francisco, CA: Jossey-Bass, 2008), 98-100.

[13] Ethical leadership and the role of followers are discussed in Joanne B. Ciulla, Ethics, the Heart of Leadership (Westport, CT: Praeger, 2014), 129-131.

[14] Collaboration between leaders and followers is emphasized in Jim Collins, Good to Great: Why Some Companies Make the Leap... and Others Don't (New York, NY: HarperBusiness, 2001), 67-69.

[15] Preparing future leaders through strong followership is explored in Warren Bennis, On Becoming a Leader (Reading, MA: Addison-Wesley, 2009), 122-124.

[16] Encouraging open communication as a part of strong followership is discussed in L. David Marquet, Turn the Ship Around!: A True Story of Turning Followers into Leaders (New York, NY: Portfolio, 2013), 156-158.

[17] Providing opportunities for growth in followership is emphasized in John C. Maxwell, The 360 Degree Leader: Developing Your Influence from Anywhere in the Organization (Nashville, TN: Thomas Nelson, 2005), 89-91.

[18] Modeling servant-hearted followership is discussed in Robert K. Greenleaf, Servant Leadership: A Journey into the Na-

ture of Legitimate Power and Greatness (Mahwah, NJ: Paulist Press, 2002), 42-44.

[19] Recognizing and affirming contributions in followership is highlighted in Gary Chapman, The 5 Languages of Appreciation in the Workplace: Empowering Organizations by Encouraging People (Chicago, IL: Northfield Publishing, 2019), 110-112.

[20] Fostering a collaborative culture between leaders and followers is discussed in Edgar H. Schein, Organizational Culture and Leadership (San Francisco, CA: Jossey-Bass, 2016), 45-47.

Follow To Lead

www.ingramcontent.com/pod-product-compliance
Lightning Source LLC
Chambersburg PA
CBHW060156130626
46556CB00006B/2667